Parting Gifts

Also by ANNE HINES,
published by McArthur & Company

A Year in HineSight

The Spiral Garden

Come Away ~ The Song of Songs

Parting Gifts

Notes on Loss, Love and Life

Anne Hines

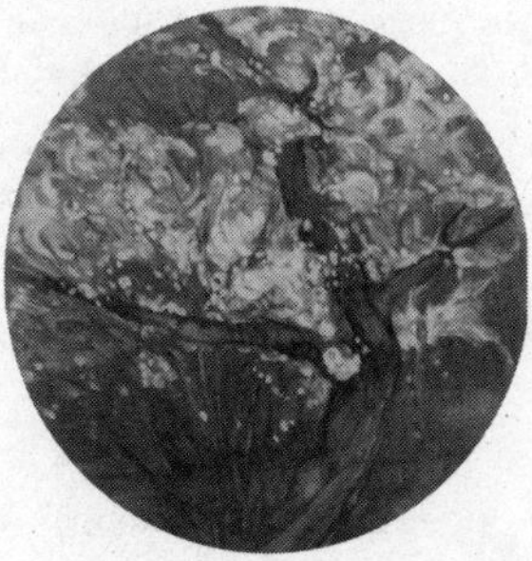

McArthur & Company
Toronto

First published in Canada in 2009 by
McArthur & Company
322 King Street West, Suite 402
Toronto, Ontario
M5V 1J2
www.mcarthur-co.com

Library and Archives Canada Cataloguing in Publication

Hines, Anne, 1958-
Parting gifts : a memoir / Anne Hines.

ISBN 978-1-55278-812-7

1. Hines, Anne, 1958-. 2. Authors, Canadian (English)—20th century—Biography. 3. Life change events. I. Title.

PS8565.I63Z472 2009 C818'.5403 C2009-904643-1

The publisher would like to acknowledge the financial support of the Government of Canada through the Book Publishing Industry Development Program (BPIDP) and the Canada Council for our publishing activities. The publisher further wishes to acknowledge the financial support of the Ontario Arts Council and the OMDC for our publishing program.

Cover painting 'Wait under the Tree' © 2009 Shinya Kumazawa
www.skartist.com

Printed and bound in Canada by Friesens

10 9 8 7 6 5 4 3 2 1

Mixed Sources
Cert no. SW-COC-001271
© 1996 FSC
FSC

To Joan Wyatt,
who inspires

CONTENTS

Introduction

This book is about loss.

In an average day, I lose my scissors, my car keys, my grocery list, my patience and my mind. In an average life, almost all of us are destined to lose our way, our bearings, our youth, our hearts and our heads.

The Buddhist masters say that life is a constant round of building up and falling away, building up and falling away. The work of life is to become as comfortable in the stages of loss and decline as we are in those of building.

This is a difficult task, made even more difficult by the fact that most of us don't want to do it. Loss begets change. And while "things change" may ironically be the only true constant in life, most of the time we'd rather fight against change than learn to accept it. The reason is obvious. Change = uncertainty. Uncertainty = queasiness. It almost always involves being wide-awake at 2 a.m. with a tension knot in your stomach the size of a bowling ball.

Loss is change writ large. And human beings are limited to three coping strategies to deal with it: acceptance, resentment or denial. Generally, we favour the last two.

A friend who practises homeopathy is convinced that resentment is the cause of cancer. I don't know about that, but I know for sure what it does cause. Deeper resentment. As a coping strategy, I don't recommend it.

Denial, on the other hand, is a nice comfortable place to be. Over many years and through many events of loss, I've turned denial into an art form.

I have said in the past that what we need are not traditional psychotherapists. The first thing a therapist wants to do is bring into the open all of the things making us anxious, where they simply make us even more anxious. What we need are denial therapists, trained professionals who can encourage us to get a good firm grip on unreality. Experts in helping us hone the skill of convincing ourselves that "it's just a slight tremour" even as the house is collapsing around us.

I have always maintained that denial therapy would work something like this:

YOU: "I'm having a problem with my mother."

DENIAL THERAPIST: "Forget about it. Have a chocolate chip cookie."

YOU: "I don't know where my life is going."

DT: "Go clean out your closet. Maybe it will go away."

At the moment, I'm dealing with changes about to be brought on by my youngest child, Becky, heading off to college. I've decided to tell myself that she's going to camp. It's a very nice camp with big tents they call "dormitories." Their first evening campfire activity is called a "keg party."

Of course, some kinds of change engender hope that both we, and our lives, will be better than before. But even when what we're losing seems to be something that really needs to be gone, there is a very real and necessary grief. When my husband, Michael, and I divorced, we expected we'd now be happier people and better co-parents. But we also knew that with divorce came the end of cherished plans and expectations.

Singly and together, we mourned the loss of those dreams. Sometimes the mourning looked like tears and sometimes it sounded like anger, but it was the same thing. We were letting go of how we thought our lives together would be and also, perhaps even more difficult, letting go of the people we'd been ourselves.

If it's true that loss is a constant of life, it is just as much the case that, in a trickle or torrent, life will always return to fill the empty space left when loss occurs. Nature abhors a vacuum. Author Helen Keller put it this way, "When one window of happiness closes, another opens. But sometimes we stand so long staring at the one that has closed, we do not see the one that has opened for us." Part of coping with loss, when the sharpest sorrow has passed, is to look for what comes to us as a result. What comes will always be different than what went before. Not better necessarily, but different. Which is OK. Because by then, we're different too.

The idea for this book occurred a few years ago when my older daughter, Jade, was getting ready to go away to college. One afternoon, I was sitting at home alone, pitying myself because my child was leaving me for the frivolous, self-indulgent pursuit of higher education. I decided I would deal with my low spirits in the usual way. I'd find something to do that would make me feel even worse. I went into Jade's bedroom and began sorting through her childhood books, grieving the infant I'd read them with who was now grown up and would soon be gone.

In spite of my plans, it turned into a lovely afternoon. I came across forgotten treasures of stories we'd laughed over together and picture books that had stirred our imaginations and swept us away to far-off lands.

Then I discovered a collection of Chinese fables that Jade had particularly loved. I flipped the book open at a story that goes like this:

A farmer goes to his barn early one morning and discovers that his horse has broken loose from its stall and run off. The man's neighbours collect around, clucking their tongues sympathetically saying, "Oh dear, truly you are an unfortunate man. What bad luck this is." The farmer shrugged his shoulders and said, "Well, maybe it is and maybe it isn't."

Later that day, the horse wanders back into the farmyard, followed by another horse. The farmer's neighbours gather around rejoicing, "Now you have two horses. What very good luck." The farmer shrugs again and says, "Well, maybe it is and maybe it's not."

The same afternoon, as he attempts to mount the new pony, the farmer's son falls off and breaks his ankle. "How unlucky!" The neighbours cry. "What terrible misfortune has been visited on your house."

The farmer answers, "Well, maybe yes and may no."

That evening, the king's guards come through the village, taking all able-bodied young men away to serve in the army. The farmer's son is left at home. The story goes on like this. You get the idea.

The point the ancient Chinese fabulist was making is that when it comes to knowing what's for the best in our lives, we don't have a clue. We think we do. We plan, save, worry and make ourselves miserable, fixating on what we believe life must look like in order for us to be happy. And yet what seems like misfortune may bring surprising gifts.

✿

About a year ago, I worked as a volunteer in a palliative care ward at a local hospital. I wasn't a natural at the job. The first day I was on duty I shattered a lightbulb in the patient lounge, set off the medic alert bell in seven of the eight rooms I visited, and almost lost one poor gentleman down a ramp by attempting to adjust his wheelchair brake as I pushed him up an incline. At the end of my shift, the floor administrator, a man famous for being prepared to tell you the exact truth about yourself, called me over. He whispered, "These people are already dying, honey. They don't need your help."

One afternoon, I sat chatting with a woman who'd come to visit her father. As he slept peacefully, she told me about the months she'd spent providing him with full-time care in his home. She'd resigned from her job, given up a senior volunteer position with a social justice agency and no longer been free to go to movies and dinner with friends.

The woman wondered if, when her father was gone, she'd be easily able to reclaim her old life and interests or if she'd have to start over, rebuilding from the ground up. I said, "This sounds like a very uncertain time for you."

The woman answered, "Well yes, but I've learned not to worry about it." She went on to explain that in addition to working and raising two sons, a part of her life had always been spent working on peace and social justice issues. She took her boys with her as she led peace rallies, helped out at a battered women's shelter and assisted at fundraising events for Amnesty International. To her horror, when they finished high school, each of her sons joined the army in order to get their university tuition paid.

"I cried," she told me. "I shouted, I coaxed, I argued. I told them I'd get a job in the evening or on weekends to help them out. Most of all, I wondered what I'd done wrong. How could my children have grown up to place so little value on peace and compassion?"

Then the war in Afghanistan began and the woman's older son was shipped overseas. She was devastated. "After all those years of working for peace, I was now in danger of having a child killed supporting a war effort."

The young man was assigned to a division whose task was going to war-devastated villages to make lists of aid resources required—food supplies, a new well, tents, medical kits. One day, his company entered a town where he noticed a group of children and adults hunched over amid the rubble of a bombed-out building, using sticks to patiently scratch figures into the hard ground. Someone said this had been a school for the blind. Most of the students had left after the school was razed, but a few had stayed on, determinedly trying to learn.

That evening, when the woman's son returned to the command post, he suggested to his fellow soldiers that their squadron "adopt" this school as a special project. The young men began spending their free time gathering bricks and rebuilding the school structure. The son telephoned home, asking his mother if she could help. "From then on," she told me excitedly, "I had whole days when I forgot he could be blown up at any minute. I was rustling up donations. Three months later, twenty-eight boxes of clothes, linens, school supplies, including Braille books, were on their way to a brand new building."

And "When my son finished his tour of duty, he switched university courses to take international relations. His goal is to work for a global aid organization some day."

When the story was finished, the woman and I sat quietly for a few minutes. The afternoon sun tinted the walls of the little hospital room a deep, rosy hue. From the street far below, we could hear the steady pulse of rush-hour traffic, keeping time with the soft, constant rhythm of her father's snoring.

Finally she said, "We don't know what's really for the best, do we? Whatever happens, there's going to be some bad in it and some good. That's what's kept me going through Dad's illness. Waiting to see the good that comes out of it."

I thought about this as I packed up Jade's old storybooks. The bad part of my children growing up and leaving I could see clearly. I would no longer be privy on a day-to-day basis to their thoughts, hopes, worries and plans.

But, as each of my children head out to take on the world, I hoped I could anticipate a great deal of good as well. I decided to jump-start the good. I got in the car and drove three boxes of books to our local Goodwill, so that they could be loved by another parent and child.

❀

This book is about losses I've experienced in life: the end of being a full-time parent, the crumbling of both my first marriage and my identity as a straight person, the loss of a son who transitioned into a daughter, an end to my faith in the God I was raised on that occurred as a result of the age-old struggle between religion and spirituality, and the conclusion of youth as I turned fifty. But mostly, it's a book about the gifts that have come into my life as a result of each loss.

A Japanese proverb says, "The barn has burned down. Now I can see the moon." Loss in life is a given. But so is the promise that from it, blessings will surely come. I've seen a lot of barns burn down in my time. I'm delighted to share this view of the moon.

—Anne Hines, Toronto, 2009

I
Losing Faith

...and Finding God

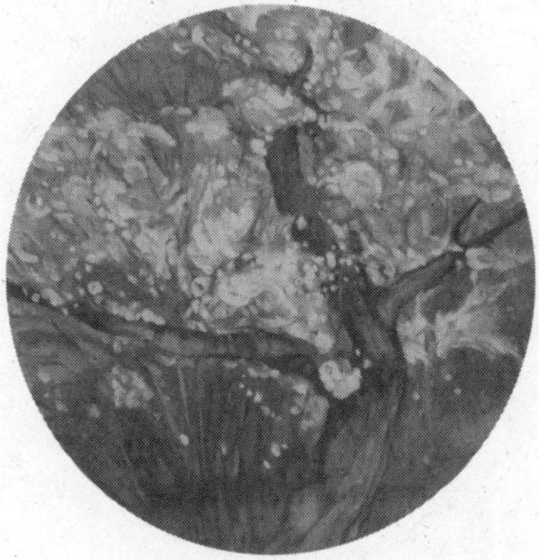

FOURTEEN YEARS AGO, I found God. As a result of this, I divorced a man, married a woman, changed careers, wrote some books, overhauled my religious beliefs, began training to become a church minister and helped a child transgender. I have come to believe that there is only one thing I know to be absolutely true: A spiritually aware life is not for sissies.

Every now and then, God points a finger at someone and says, "You. Now." And that person's life is changed forever.

I don't know why God singles some people out in this way. For most of my life, all I knew about God talking to people was that you wanted to avoid having it happen to you.

Take the Apostle Paul, for example. For those readers who are unfamiliar with the Christian scriptures I should explain that the Bible is divided into two sections called the Old Testament and New Testament. The Old Testament could also be entitled "God," followed by the New Testament sequel, "Son of God." Jesus figures very big in the second part, as does the Apostle Paul.

Paul, who was called Saul at the time, was making his way along the Damascus Road outside Jerusalem one day, just going about his business, which happened to be persecuting members of an annoying new upstart religious sect called "Christianity." Suddenly, God looked down and said, "Hey, Saul. You. Now."

Paul was temporarily struck blind. Then God started to talk to him. We are not entirely sure what God said, but the result of this event was that Paul instantly changed his name and became a convert to the very same small, annoying, practically illegal upstart religious sect he'd been working so hard to snuff out. He spent the rest of his life bickering with fellow church members, running afoul of his bosses—the guys running the Jesus franchise in Jerusalem, dashing off letters that alternated between out-and-out whining and phrases so glorious you'd think angels were guiding his pen, all the while trying to avoid being arrested and/or killed by the people he himself used to work for. This last part goes particularly badly. Paul lands in jail where he dies alone and largely unappreciated.

When I was taught this story as a child in Sunday School, we were told that the message of Paul's experience is that we should "Let God guide your life." I, for one, was thinking, "Ho no, boy. Not me."

Of course there have been people who were visited by God and who fared better. Joan of Arc...well no, she was burned at the stake. Saint Peter...died horribly in jail.

Saint Agatha...was arrested, whipped, interned in a brothel, rolled over hot coals and went mad—possibly not in that exact order.

Mother Teresa. She heard God talk to her while on a train on her way to a spiritual retreat. Teresa didn't go mad. She didn't die in jail. Nothing traumatic happened to Teresa at all. In fact, she won the Nobel Prize for Peace and passed away serenely, surrounded by adoring adherents, her name universally synonymous with selfless love and her work having inspired people around the world. Mind you, this was after living in almost unimaginably Spartan conditions, bedding down on the bare floor, washing in glacial water from an outdoor pump and eating one meagre meal a day, all the while ministering to dying lepers in the most squalid slums on earth.

I admire Joan of Arc. I'm impressed by the life of Saint Peter. I revere Mother Teresa. I do not actually wish to be any one of them. What I want is to sit comfortably at home, grateful that there are people such as Joan of Arc and Mother Teresa in the world and that I'm not one of them. My reaction to hearing stories of such people as an adult was not so different to what it was as a child. "How selfless. How inspiring. But, ho no, boy. Not me."

The experience of all these people proves that those who are visited by God end up having to change their lives in all kinds of difficult and uncomfortable ways. Viewing a site where Jesus or the Virgin Mary is reported to have appeared is probably the most that should be attempted, since the danger is past. But actually being visited by God yourself, hearing God speak to you, probably not to say, "Everything is fine the way it is. You might want to think about changing up the colours of those throw pillows in the living room, but otherwise, just keep doing what you're doing," should be avoided like all get-out. From childhood until my late thirties, the lesson was clear. If you don't want to live a life of upheaval, hardship and bad sleeping conditions, do not get too close to God.

The religion I grew up with understood this entirely. Philosopher Carl Jung claimed, "Religion is a defence against a religious experience." At our church, we saw this as a good thing. "Avoid firsthand encounters with the divine" could have been our organizational mission statement.

In our church we insisted, in fact, that God does not speak to people directly anymore. No one was really sure why this was. It was just generally felt that we simply no longer lived in times where miracles such as visitations occur. And that this is just as well.

Just because God doesn't speak to us didn't mean we shouldn't speak to God. In our church we carried on a kind of continual earnest soliloquy common to many mainstream faith paths. We talked to God, called on God, petitioned God and praised God. We quoted God. We read the Bible and memorized huge passages of it. I was the unbeaten star of our Sunday School scripture recitation competitions. There wasn't a Noah's Ark finger puppet set or white calfskin Bible with embossed gold lettering and the actual, real words said by Jesus printed in red ink that I didn't walk away with. That I kept my head in spite of all this success still amazes me.

There were a lot of good things about my church. The people of my church family were thoughtful and caring. The ladies knitted mittens for Native children and held bake sales in aid of Bolivian orphans. When someone was sick or had a loved one pass away, our churchwomen were the first to arrive, bearing casseroles and kind words. We looked after each other and tried also to look after the rest of the world as best we could. Being part of that church family taught me valuable lessons in how to live gently and generously with others.

What I didn't learn to do was to listen. There was a general feeling that people who listened to God and who claimed to hear something in return were, to put it kindly, a little nuts. Or else they were headed for a heap of trouble, like Saint Paul. Neither of these were desirable things to be in an orderly suburban Protestant church.

In place of God making personal appearances, the church was prepared to take on the job of telling us what God would have said, had God actually spoken, without the danger of our being frightened out of our wits or having to alter our life plans in any inconvenient or unsettling ways. Mostly, our church assured us that what God wanted was for us to stick to the program and maintain the status quo. If we did this, God would ensure that nothing bad would happen.

✿

This image of God reminds me of a joke:

The head of marketing for a major burger chain telephones the Pope one day and says, "Your holiness, we here at Burgers R Us have a proposition for you. We've heard that your people have a prayer you say all the time. It goes something like, 'Our father who art in heaven...yadda, yadda, yadda...' and then, 'Give us this day, our daily bread.' Your worshipfulness, Burgers R Us is prepared to offer your church fifty million dollars if you'll just change the wording to, 'Give us this day our daily hamburger.'"

Well, of course the Pope was incensed. He was so outraged and offended he could hardly speak. Finally he managed to sputter, "Sir, you are talking about our Church's most sacred prayer. The words to this prayer were taught to us by Christ himself. We are not going to change it to 'Give us our daily burger.' Goodbye." And the Pope hangs up.

A week later the head of marketing telephones the Pope again. He says, "Your Godliness, the boys and I have been talking it over and we realize that the deal we offered you was totally insulting. But I have a figure now I think you're really going to go for."

An hour later the Pope calls an emergency meeting of all the cardinals. He stands before them in the Sistine Chapel and announces, "Gentlemen, I have some good news and some bad news. The good news is, I've got a way we can make a hundred million dollars for the Church. The bad news is, we're going to have to get out of our contract with Dempsters."

Growing up, I came to think of God as signatory to one-half of a grand metaphysical contract. Nothing I heard or read or memorized from the Bible did anything to challenge this idea one bit. Moses agreed to obey God, in return for which he got a Promised Land. David agreed to obey God, in return for which he got to be king. Jesus obeyed God, in return for which he died horribly on a cross, but almost right after that he got to ascend into heaven and help run things.

The moral was clear. Behave well and God would ensure that nothing very bad would ever happen. If it did it must have been because I hadn't kept up my end of the bargain. This was basic traditional theology that would have served me well in life had it not been for one minor wrinkle. To my mind, it has nothing to do with what God is really like.

The first cracks in this image of God appeared when I was a young teen. I began to feel that though the terms of the "behaving well" contract were always clearly spelled out, they were not always clearly rational. In fact, God appeared to me to care about some very odd things. For instance, God really didn't like us to wear nail polish in church. I remember standing among the choir on Sunday morning, anxiously tipping my hymn book forward, hoping that no one had glimpsed my fingertips. Any sighting of Kitten Pink or Peach Passion, and the elderly ladies in the front pews would be squabbling during the sermon over who got to share the news with my mother during Fellowship Hour.

God also did not want us to go to movies on Sunday. God didn't think we should go to our local fall fair on the Sabbath either. Apparently watching pumpkin-rolling races or checking out who won prizes for "pictures of famous landmarks rendered entirely in sunflower seeds" inhibited spiritual flowering. God didn't like us to dance or listen to rock music or any other kind of music we really enjoyed. A non-churchgoing friend, who found this almost as incomprehensible as I, told me this joke: "Why don't Baptists approve of having sex standing up?" The answer was, "They're afraid it might lead to dancing." To me this just proved how ignorant secularists were. Everyone knew God didn't approve of sex of any kind.

God definitely didn't think we should have sex before marriage. At least I was given a reason for this one. A Sunday School teacher explained carefully and clearly to our teen class that if people went around having sex prior to marriage it would rip asunder the very fabric of our social order, plunging humankind into chaos and exposing us, every one, to the naked wrath of God. She was quite sure of it.

The merit of this argument was, of course, its long tradition. "If this happens, the world will end," has been used to warn against everything from speaking disrespectfully of Zeus to legalizing same-sex marriage. To me, the problem with this rationale is that the world doesn't end. It simply changes. Which seems a proper thing for it to do.

The "no sex before wedlock" expectation was reasonable back in the days when sexual maturity was followed closely by marriage. But now, we expect young people to wait several years before marrying, until they finish college or university and establish careers. A God who continued to insist on the same rules and demand I postpone intimacy a good ten, even fifteen, years longer than any previous generation, seemed not only irrational but downright cruel. As outrageous as...well, a God who thought the most sensible way to save the world from sin was by nailing his son to a cross. I didn't understand that either. And it didn't take a theological genius to look around and see that if that was God's intent, it apparently didn't take.

It was never explained why God decreed all these things, but the message seemed clear. At worst, God was an unreasoning tyrant. At best, God didn't want us to have any fun.

God didn't want us to get chummy with the Catholics either. I was astounded when I got to university and was told by my Catholic roommate that she'd been assured that God frowned on her palling around with Protestants.

What I slowly began to realize was that where religious practice is concerned, logic is often not invited to the planning table. Take the medieval age, for example. This is a period of history spanning roughly AD 400 to 1250. During this time, Christianity was at the height of its power and influence. But frankly, for the Church, this could well have been known as "the silly season."

At one point, opposing factions in Rome elected two different candidates as Pope at the same time. One was headquartered in Rome, the other based in Avignon. Each warring side of Church leaders claimed their man to be the one chosen by God to uphold his laws of peace and compassion. These duelling pontiffs, meanwhile, spent most of their time and energy as spiritual leaders attempting to poison each other.

Also in medieval times, priests went about whacking themselves on the forehead with planks believing that, if they suffered enough by their own effort, God could leave off punishing the world with plagues. Spiritual pilgrims swarmed Europe and the Holy Land, prostrating themselves in front of bone fragments reputed to have belonged to various saints, on display at many churches. Owning a relic was a coup for any house of religion, bringing not only fame, but also funds from the crowds surging through towns and countryside, eager to revere the third toe of Saint Peter or a sliver of the ulna of the Virgin Mary. The fact that, according to the teachings of this same Church, Mary had been taken bodily and whole up into heaven didn't lessen devotees' enthusiasm one jot. As late as the 1400s, one priest noted that there were enough remnants of the jawbone of John the Baptist to make up several skulls. At least one of these, he knew for certain, was actually a hunk of pumice stone.

The unreasonableness of religious practice in medieval times, and in most if not all religions before or after, speaks to two realities. First, when it comes to finding meaning and connection in our lives, we're willing to try anything. Second, the aim of religion is not to be reasonable or logical. The aim of religion is to make God manageable. This may, in fact, be the most unreasonable, illogical undertaking of all.

What my well-intentioned church and equally well-meaning Sunday School teachers were trying to do was to keep me safe. And, as these people who had read the stories of Saint Paul well knew, the only possible way to achieve this would be to pen the divine in, limiting it to a role as a kind of patron saint of Seeing That Nothing Ever Changes. If God can be wrestled into limited belief systems and a few carefully chosen images instead of being known through dangerous, unpredictable personal experience, then maybe we'd never suffer the trials of Saint Paul or Mother Teresa and be called on to open our minds to all sorts of startling new ideas, or to change our lives forever in uncomfortable and disturbing ways. When God is fenced in, we are safe.

To keep God fenced in it's necessary to engage in some serious God-wrangling. Fortunately, organized religious groups are usually highly skilled at this.

God-wrangling is the act of trying to confine the divine to neatly defined doctrines, in an attempt to make God tame and predictable. With a little determined God-wrangling, the divine becomes something that may be contained in a few dry bones, or a few dusty ancient pages of scripture or almost equally ancient and even dustier laws and definitions.

The problem with God-wrangling is that it means institutionalized religion is often a lousy place to find God. There is a story that one day, a fellow traveller confronted a tenth-century monk on the road to a meeting of church leaders in Rome. The man was eager to live a more spiritually connected life. He asked the monk if he believed that the priests of the Holy City were uniquely blessed men and whether the Orthodox Church of Rome was truly the one and only place to find God. In response, the monk is reputed to have shook his head sadly and coined this rhyme, "If in Rome, you have sought Him/You won't find Him, unless you've brought Him."

God-wrangling has been a staple of church activity since there was church. The earliest Christians, when they had a moment free from worrying about being ridiculed, jailed or tossed to the lions, spent most of it arguing over what was the proper way to speak of and approach God.

Containing God is a very big task. Some of the greatest minds in history have dedicated themselves to creating the rules and doctrines that make it seem possible. Some of the mightiest armies in history have dedicated themselves to wiping out those who either didn't agree with these rules and definitions or who didn't see making God manageable as a good thing. Religion is and has always been mankind's most effective weapon of mass destruction.

✿

The most critical, fundamental key to successful God-wrangling is learning not to listen. Listening is an act of radical courage. It's the same whether you're dealing with God or another human being. Listening demands contact instead of contracts. It transforms rules into relationship. Talking is entirely safe. You'll only ever say things you already know. There's nothing safe about listening.

There is a catch to this "don't listen/don't hear," keeping-God-small approach to the divine. Trying to limit the divine spirit is like trying to stop up water from a broken dike. Whatever this "other" thing is—this creator, this Tao, goddess, Supreme Being, presence, this energy that we believe cares about us and our troubles—it will not be contained. The god thing pushes through the cracks in our fortress walls of religious doctrine, cascades down through chinks and gaps, blossoming into the air as fresh and feral as spring. It snakes tendril vines of longing and promise around our still, safe hearts, promising wanton joy.

One day, we may find ourselves wondering if not hearing what the god thing has to say is too high a price to pay for safety. Then, a voice within murmurs that safety is a dream and perhaps we'd like to wake up now, smell the celestial coffee and join in the real life happening all around. And sometimes, if we are very lucky, we can't help but hear.

When I grew up and went away to university, I stopped going to church. I'd had it up the wazoo with the basic tenet of God-wrangling, the divine's primary agreement with humankind, "Toe the line. Behave yourself and God won't let anything bad happen." The fact was I was now regularly flouting God's dictates with such depraved practices as going to the movies on Sunday and fraternizing with my Papist roommate. There didn't seem to be any point in attending church services and reviewing the contract, given that I was regularly defaulting on the terms.

Then I married Michael, who came from a background that was solidly non-partisan where religion was concerned, but agreed that, when we became parents, we should take our children to Sunday School. Having children to raise suddenly made "Toe the line" seem like a very fair and useful message to be sharing. Besides, attendance at church would help instill some good, wholesome, middle-class family values in our offspring.

When our first child was born I shopped around and finally hit on a church I thought would suit us. I invited the minister for a family visit during which he and Michael talked about golf for an hour. The subject of God never came up. Afterward, Michael said he was pleased we'd found a faith group he could relate to. I felt the same.

We started to go to church with our first child, then, when Becky was born, with a second in tow. Michael, who is a fine musician, played guitar and sang at special services. I taught Sunday School and helped organize the annual rummage sale. We attended social events and gave donations. It was all pretty much like the church experience I'd had as a child. Each Sunday I sat in the pew, repeated the standard prayers and sang the approved hymns, reassured by divinity made manageable. I was entirely content to buy into the premise that so long as I was maintaining the status quo, God, in turn, would make sure nothing bad ever happened.

Life went along fairly smoothly until April 16, 1994. On April 16, 1994, I found out that God-wrangling doesn't work. God will not be contained.

❀

Friedrich Nietzsche was a philologist, born in Germany in the mid-1800s. He abandoned being a philologist, possibly upon realizing that no one knew what a philologist was. He then turned his mind to studying and writing poetry and theology, which are pretty much the same thing. He ended up saying some very smart things.

Among these, Nietzsche said that if a person is going to suffer a significant spiritual crisis it is most likely to occur in their middle to late thirties. Mother Teresa was around that age the day she heard God speak to her while on a train heading to a religious retreat. On April 16, 1994, I was that age too. This is pretty much where any similarity between Mother Teresa and I ends. Except that for both of us, God looked down, pointed a finger in our direction and said, "You. Now." And nothing would ever be the same.

❀

It had begun the fall before. I quit my job. Actually, I only quit one of my two jobs. I had a stressful, demanding nine-to-five job running a theatre company and a more stressful, demanding five-to-nine job running after my kids. My life had got to the stage where I could no longer maintain full-time paid work, full-time parenting work and my sanity all at the same time. For a while, like most women, I felt I could just do without sanity. Much the same way as I'd learned to do without muscle tone, personal space, and breaks to use the bathroom. The day I caught myself yelling at an actor that if he ever delivered his opening line that way again, he wasn't getting dessert for a week, I realized that sanity might be a necessary commodity after all. One of my jobs had to go. Since there are laws about opting out of parenthood, I decided to quit working at the theatre. Friends told me I'd be crazy within six months. They were wrong. It only took three.

The way I look at it now, becoming an at-home mother for me was about as easy a transition as an Olympic swimmer suddenly being confined to a wading pool. I felt imprisoned. Frustrated. Trapped. I loved my kids. I just didn't always love being a parent.

Here I was, constantly, relentlessly, twenty-four-hours-a-day, in the company of my children, now aged four and seven, the two people I loved most in the world, and I'd never felt more alone. I felt starved for connection with the world outside of *Sesame Street* and Kindergym. There were days when the longest conversation I had with an adult was when I said "thank you" to a grocery store clerk for giving me my change.

There were upsides, of course. Being a stay-at-home mother meant that people no longer pestered me at dinner parties, wanting to know my opinion on anything. I didn't have the daily chore of deciding where or what to have for lunch, my options being pretty much limited to "whatever's in the fridge that the kids won't eat." And there was always someone who wanted to be with me. Every single moment. Wherever I went. A friend told me that she purposely did the worst household chores—cleaning the toilets, taking out the garbage—when her kids were driving her nuts so they'd leave her alone for a few minutes. She said, "One day I was elbow deep, stirring the rancid glop in the bottom of the compost bin, thinking how great it was to have a moment to myself. It suddenly occurred to me that this was not really how I'd pictured my life turning out."

There is an old saying, "It takes a village to raise a child." I began to think it should read, "It takes a village to keep a stay-at-home mother from clubbing her children to death." Most days all that saved me, and them, was having my own mother to call for support. My mother once told me that in March of a particularly long, nasty winter, she was so desperate for adult company that she spent over an hour one day packing every one of her then four kids into their snowsuits, boots, hats and mitts, preparing to walk next door to visit a neighbour. "By the time I got you all ready," she said, "I was too exhausted to go anywhere."

I knew I was lucky to have the choice to be home with my kids, but I missed making decisions bigger than whether to change brands of pudding cups. I wanted to be asked my advice about...anything. I wanted to wander by a colleague's desk with a cup of coffee and chat about how their weekend had been. I wanted to wear clothes whose biggest selling point was not that they didn't show stains.

Most of all, I wanted to know who I was now. Like many people, I had known who I was by my job. This was foolish of course. Worth and identity are not determined by your job. They're determined by your job title.

For example, say what you do on a given day is to referee eighteen hundred squabbles, keep everyone you're responsible for working to deadline, make sure they've all got what they need when they need it so they can do whatever it is they need to do, all the while putting on a good face for the world, claiming that everything is going along swimmingly and that, truly, you're not living in a state of constant outright chaos. That night you attend a dinner party where someone asks, "So, what do you do?" And you answer either, "I'm CEO of a major software marketing firm" or "I'm at home with my kids." Only one of these titles will solicit the proper impressed response. The job is pretty much the same.

Poet Pablo Neruda said, "All paths lead to the same goal: to convey to others what we are." I quit my job and suddenly, I had no idea who I was. I knew who I was in connection with other people. I was Jade and Becky's mother, Michael's wife, Otha's daughter. But what title was there that connected me to myself?

Having a paid job was troublesome but having the job title had been useful. It was an easy answer to "Who am I?" I was "a crazy, stressed person who ran around like mad every second of the day trying to keep afloat a not-for-profit theatre company and care for a spouse, two kids and a few extended family members and who, given fifteen minutes of unscheduled time, spent it wondering if it was enough to get to the dry cleaner, pick up kitty litter and take back the library books, or if I should just pass on the litter one more time and hope they'd keep pooping on the old carpet downstairs and not the new upstairs one that I'd just had cleaned."* It wasn't a

* Note to cat-loving readers: I took good care of our two cats, which lived healthy lives until they were eighteen and seventeen. I only failed to pick up the litter once. Truly. Please don't leave messages on my website.

great answer, but it was an answer.

Now when I asked myself, "Who am I?" not in relation to my family or my household, but just to me, I wasn't so sure.

There is no greater loneliness than being without connection to our own Self. Years ago, Mother Teresa was invited to speak to a graduating class at Harvard Law School. She told the faculty and students that, while the people in the slums of Calcutta struggle with extreme physical poverty, when she comes to North America she feels overwhelmed by the poverty she sees everywhere in our society. The poverty of loneliness. The staff and students of Harvard Law School dissolved into tears. It was this loneliness that crushed down on me now, a deep, persistent ache resulting from not knowing myself, meaning I could never be known by anyone else. Feeling severed from my soul meant, just as surely, that I felt equally cut off from all those around me.

I decided the best way to deal with the realization that I had no idea who I was, was simply to apply the method I used for all other difficult and pressing personal problems. I would try avoiding it altogether.

I turned on the radio. I ran errands. I read newspapers and magazines full of information that was vital to the world and that I'd forget an hour later. I filled my mind with noise, just as we used to fill up our church services with singing and talking and praying, anything that would keep us from having to hear.

The radio and TV, obligations and sheer outright fatigue were enough to keep the loneliness at bay. For a while, I managed to avoid the all-important, "Who am I?"

The universe however thinks "Who am I?" is a fine question for us to be asking. It devises ways to get our attention. When it comes to making us face up to the big issues of life, the Powers That Be pull out all the stops. They give us four o'clock in the afternoon.

Four o'clock in the afternoon is, to quote the late Douglas Adams, "the Long Dark Teatime of The Soul." It's too late in the day to start new projects yet too early to begin the tasks of evening. Four o'clock in the afternoon has neither the demands of noontide nor the consolation of evening.

When I was working outside the home I was too distracted to notice the pathos of four o'clock. Late afternoon meant it was time to hustle through my last few paid duties before racing to the car, careening to the grocery store, grabbing something that could be served up and would look like dinner, then barrelling home to start my second, unpaid job. Four o'clock could have hit me over the head with pathos and I'd barely have noticed.

Now, I was home at four o'clock. Four o'clock was just after I'd picked up the kids from school. Sometimes we had music or skating lessons to get to, but if not, this was an in-between time of day. Our lives outside the house were done for the day, the approaching busyness of dinner and bedtime not yet quite upon us.

I would sit at the kitchen table with a cup of tea that always seemed half finished. The kids would be watching TV or happily squabbling over the Nintendo.

When I first began this ritual of sitting and doing nothing, amber autumn light drifted through the sliding doors that look out at my tiny city backyard, illuminating the fine dust on the kitchen floor. In the weeks that followed, rain trickled snail paths down the windows. Then, snow billowed like ocean waves against the glass.

There are two times when you should never contemplate your life, but it's all you can do. One is two o'clock in the morning. The other, four o'clock in the afternoon. I would sit alone at the kitchen table. Loneliness would swarm around me like persistent children, screeching, "Who am I?" tearing at my heart with cries for comfort.

I understood why some stay-at-home mothers drink. And why mothers at my kids' school casually referred to Prozac as "Vitamin P." When you're not out in the world, it's harder to keep from hearing those big questions. It's difficult not to fall prey to the despair of knowing that we are, each of us, deeply and profoundly alone. In the long, lonely twilight afternoon of the spirit, sitting at the kitchen table before a cup of tea that may never be finished, the truth is impossible to escape. No wonder *Oprah*, a television show that dishes out care and companionship, comes on at that hour of the afternoon. It's a suicide prevention program.

Friedrich Nietzsche, the man who said that a spiritual crisis is most likely to happen in our thirties, knew what it was for a person to yearn for connection with his soul. I think Nietzsche must have owned a kitchen table. And I suspect he sat there over more than a few cups of tea.

Nietzsche said the reason a spiritual crisis may occur in our late thirties is because at that point we have time to take a breath and think about what we truly want out of life. Perhaps our late thirties and early forties are the four o'clock of a lifetime. The busiest years are, to some extent, behind us. But the end of our day is still a long way off.

In middle age, many of us do pause and tally up what we've gained thus far. Perhaps by now, we've got the job, the spouse, the house, the kids and the car. It's time to consider what comes next. And for many of us, what we realize is that we're not entirely sure. We feel a certain disappointment. Then emptiness. Something is missing. We begin to long for whatever it might be that would make us truly fulfilled.

It's at precisely this point, Nietzsche suggests, when something extraordinary may occur. We may lose faith with the promises of the world, start to doubt that unspoken contract that if we marry and have children, get the house, then the bigger house and then the car with tinted windows, then the car with the tinted windows, heated seats and GPS, amass fame, fortune and a solid retirement plan, that this will satisfy us entirely. And when that happens, when doubt in the promise becomes too great to ignore, we experience a full-blown crisis of spirit. Sometimes we call this an identity crisis. Whatever you call it, it means having no idea who you are or what might be found that could fill that gaping space of loneliness within.

After about three months of being a stay-at-home mother, three months of endless, solitary cups of tea and communion-craving four o'clocks, I started to notice some changes in my behaviour. As a general assessment, I would describe these behaviours as "extremely alarming" or, alternatively, "mind-bogglingly terrifying."

✿

One of my responsibilities at the theatre company I'd worked for had been to write plays. I penned my first play when the professional playwright we'd hired called me weeks before rehearsal to announce he was suffering a bout of creative anxiety and didn't feel up to actually producing a script. Not having money or time to hire a replacement, I realized I'd have to write the play myself.

What followed was like something out of an old movie in which the star is suddenly taken ill or hobbled or is otherwise unable to perform and the understudy is shoved on at the last minute, decked out in a fabulous gown, wafting onto the stage into instant success and acclaim. In my case, I didn't get to be decked out or do any wafting. And I don't recall anything more than modest approval from the audience when the show "hit the boards." What I do remember is being hunched over a computer keyboard for three weeks, rumpled, sweaty, intermittently damning to hell all temperamental playwrights and their kind. It wouldn't have made much of a movie. But the momentous conclusion was, I found out I liked to write.

When I left the theatre company, I had an idea I'd try my hand at other kinds of writing, maybe short stories. Given what I know now, this was a foolish idea.

Having worked as a writer for many years it's my observation that people generally write whatever genre they read. At the time, I hadn't read many short stories. I didn't particularly like short stories. Thinking I could pen an acceptable short story after reading only one or two was akin to someone thinking they'd make an excellent swimmer because they'd once seen the ocean.

To write with any competence, you must immerse yourself in the writing style. Not just stick in a big toe to test the waters or roll up the trouser bottoms and splash about a bit, but plunge in deep, soak long, chart the course of the currents. You must savour the tone of the words like the tang of salt on your tongue. Learn the murky dangers and buoyant joys.

The short story I wrote was very, very bad. Actually, having just paused to drag it out of my files and give it another once over, I would now say, it was not very, very bad. With intelligent editing, a structural overhaul and a complete reworking of the main characters it could possibly, with work, become very, very bad. At present, it is worse than that. It is to the genre of short stories what *Gidget Goes Hawaiian* is to the world of dramatic filmmaking.

After that first failed attempt, I wrote half a story and abandoned it. Then I wrote a few paragraphs of a story. Then just an opening line. After that, I couldn't turn on the computer. Then I couldn't go into the room where the computer was. I began to think something was up.

If I couldn't write, I decided I would be productive in some other way. I would apply myself to housework. I found I couldn't bring myself to do the laundry. What was even stranger was that I would have liked to have done the laundry. Perhaps it would take my mind off that disturbing question that was constantly elbowing its way into my consciousness. But I felt paralyzed when I went near the laundry room.

Then, I couldn't dust or vacuum. I wanted to dust and vacuum. Mostly because when I didn't dust or vacuum I found myself sitting at the window in the kitchen with that half-finished cup of tea on the table in front of me. When that happened, I was unable to avoid hearing the persistent inner voice, demanding that I do something about this crush of loneliness and start forging some sort of connection with myself. I couldn't do it. I had no idea who that was.

As the weeks passed, I found I could no longer shop for groceries or cook. I have no idea what we ate but I'm sure that I didn't make it. Not only was I not connected to my inner Self, I couldn't seem to connect any longer with the world around me. I couldn't clean or remember to fill out school forms or to call the plumber to fix that really annoying drip in the bathroom. The only thing I could still do was look after the kids. There's some kind of mother gene, I think, that enables us to watch out for our children even when we've lost sight of ourselves.

I picked the kids up from school, took them to their

activities, made sure they were fed and washed and safely tucked into bed, then got them up and dropped them off at school once more. When I had done that, I would come home, sit down at the kitchen table and...well, that was about it. The four o'clock emptiness now permeated every hour. For days, I sat down at that table and went into a kind of suspended animation until it was time to go pick the kids up again, bring them home, feed them, wash them, put them to bed and get ready to do it all over the next morning.

Wherever I went, loneliness in the form of a question pressed against my muddled mind as I stumbled through the few activities I could manage in my day. When I sat in church it raged at me. It bellowed to be attended to as I tried to chat with friends over coffee or struggled to concentrate during parent/teacher meetings. I felt almost compelled to say, "I'm sorry, can you repeat what you said about Becky needing to improve her fingerpainting skills? I'm rather distracted by the feeling of being adrift in a spiritually desolate universe." The teacher, who must have been used to dealing with parents in their late-thirties, likely wouldn't have batted an eye.

My mother suspected something was wrong and suggested we go out for lunch and shopping. The voice inside screamed. I was afraid other people in the mall would hear. I said maybe another time.

Michael awoke one night, realized I wasn't in bed and came downstairs to find me sitting in the front-hall closet. I'd had an idea that perhaps if I got into the closet, the thing that was demanding an answer would stay outside the closet and I could stay inside and we simply wouldn't have anything more to do with each other.

Michael and I went back to bed. He suggested, quite reasonably, that sitting in a closet in the middle of the night didn't seem to be something an entirely happy, well-adjusted person would do. He asked if there was anything he could do to help.

I said that perhaps what I needed was a hobby. *"Something to take my mind off the fact that I'm entirely disassociated from my true Self."* I said I thought scrapbooking might be pleasant. Michael suggested this might not be the best time to be using scissors and a glue gun. This, in fact, was helpful.

I went to see a psychiatrist. I said I didn't know what was wrong with me. I had everything I had ever been told was important. I went through the list. "I have a terrific husband, wonderful kids, a great house, financial security, friends, family..." The psychiatrist said, "Maybe you're one of those people who just can't be happy." This was not so helpful. Years later, I would realize that what she should have said was, "Hmm...perhaps you're working with the wrong list."

The psychiatrist suggested antidepressants. I have nothing against antidepressants. But I didn't want to just dull the pain. I wanted an answer to my question.

Being a churchgoing person, I might have expected to find rescue in religion. Frankly, I was not finding I had much truck with God in those days. I was living up to my end of the contract after all. I had got married, had children and tried to behave decently to my fellow human beings, with the possible, and really understandable exceptions of telemarketers and a few relatives. In return, God was supposed to invest my life with blessedness, light and meaning. At the very least he ought to be keeping me from wanting to sit in closets.

I had fulfilled my part of the deal. God had reneged. In the great ocean that is life, I was not being saved from floundering. God wasn't paddling over the horizon, leaning out of a lifeboat saying, "Oh, are you in trouble? Sorry, I hadn't noticed."

Either God didn't exist, didn't care or was fully occupied trying to sort out larger issues than my crisis of identity. In any case, it seemed pretty clear that the God I'd been raised with wasn't about to show up and pull me out of the drink of despair into which I was quickly sinking.

By April 16, 1994, the thing screeching inside me, wailing out its insistence to be heard and named and comforted had become so loud, I could barely hear what was going on around me. I could no longer count on the television, radio, housework or any other sound or activity to distract me from the voice within, keening in despair. On April 16, 1994, I told myself that I couldn't live like this any longer.

Writer and poet Sylvia Plath said that once you have children, suicide is out of the question. Then she stuck her head in a gas oven. On the afternoon of April 16, I began to wonder if that was the answer.

I took the kids back to school after lunch, the mother gene allowing me to remember that Jade needed her library books and to give Becky the bag with the pictures of bears we'd cut out of *National Geographic* the previous evening. I came home. I didn't go and sit at the kitchen table. I went into the living room. In my mind, I was begging for help. Pleading. *"If there is anyone, anything there at all, anywhere, please, please help me."* Be it God, angels, Christ or the devil himself. I wasn't feeling very particular anymore.

I got down on my hands and knees in the middle of the living-room carpet. The terror of the last few weeks, of not having an answer to that most vital question welled up from soul to heart to throat.

I howled. Loudly. Agonizingly. With all I had in me.

I howled as a wolf howls in the depths of the cold, barren wastes of winter. I howled the pain of being human and profoundly solitary and of being separated from my own soul. I screamed out the horror of having no idea who I might be. I cried out my anger that the God of contracts did not hold and could not help me or stop me from falling. I wailed out every last vestige of longing, hope or fear. Until I had nothing left inside. Not even the bleak anguish of being alone.

I stopped howling when I became too exhausted to breathe. Too exhausted even to be frightened by my own actions.

I limped upstairs, sank down into an old armchair in the small room where I had tried to write and thought, "There is nothing left."

I was empty. I was empty of the will to fight any longer. Empty also of ideas about what I wanted or what my life ought to look like. And depleted of any thoughts about who I might be. The question "Who am I?" remained. But I was devoid of both the desire and the energy to pursue an answer.

I thought, "That's it. There is nothing left in me. There is nothing." Not even enough sense of my own existence to end it.

And then I heard a voice. As if a person standing next to me now leaned close over my shoulder and tenderly, clearly and audibly began to speak.

The voice said, "Now we can begin."

To this day, I don't know what finally caused the universe to intervene. Either the howls of my soul were so loud they were at last heard in heaven, or the tendrils squeezing my still heart pulled so tightly, coaxing it into new life, they had caused it to burst. Or, perhaps the god thing had simply been waiting for me to exhaust my own efforts to steer my life. Perhaps the universe had been giving me time and space to realize that what we call strength is often just stubbornness and fear. It could be, in fact, that the divine was waiting for me to finally opt out of our contract so that we could enter into an actual relationship.

What I do know is that, in that moment, God looked down, pointed a finger in my direction and said clearly and audibly, "You. Now." And then, "Now we can begin." As it turned out, I was right about what happens to people God speaks to. Nothing would ever be the same again.

I write this, many years later, sitting in the same small room, and it sounds ludicrous. Howling. God speaking. As clearly as a person standing so close, that I not only heard the words, I felt the rush of soft warm breath they were carried on. These things don't happen to normal people. Wolf-howling and God-hearing are the sorts of things experienced by people such as apostles or saints or the guy who lives in the alley behind the beer store and who keeps an extensive collection of used cigarette papers and twine.

✿

At the time, I realized this could only mean one thing. I had lost my mind. I was insane. But perhaps that was OK. Losing my mind was a small price to pay for finding myself. And encountering God is not, after all, a sane act. Which does not mean for a moment we shouldn't attempt it. What wonderful things did reason and rationality ever get us, anyway? Political systems. Wars. Parking meters.

I had tried behaving reasonably. I had ended up in a closet. Possibly insanity was the better way to go.

✿

Nature abhors a vacuum. God, on the other hand, sees it as an excellent place to start. Having been emptied out of everything, including my belief about whether or not there is a god thing and if it still speaks to people, and ideas about what life ought to look like, new thoughts began to flood the empty space.

I realized that, except for what happens when God speaks, I was wrong about everything else. This was a good thing. It reminded me of a poem by Yehuda Amichai that goes, "From the places where we are right/flowers will never grow in the spring…But doubts and loves dig up the world/like a mole, a plough." The hard-packed psychic soil that needed digging up was my rock-solid belief that I knew what my life should look like and what I needed in order to be happy. I now had serious doubts about this. I wondered if with, "Now we may begin," the Universe was indicating it felt I was now prepared to accept suggestions.

I got out of the chair. I let my life begin to teach me.

I noted what people said to me in passing. I read the books that fell into my hands. I listened respectfully to what notions occurred as I went for long walks in sun-speckled parks. There is an old saying, "When the student is ready, the teacher appears." I decided this could also be understood as, "When the student is entirely flummoxed and has no idea who she is or what she's supposed to learn, the sound of the wind itself may teach her."

I realized that if I wanted life to be different, as in not leading to more closet-sitting or wolf-howling, then I was going to have to make some different life choices. What I needed was a new list.

I began to inventory every choice I'd made. I asked, "Do I want this? Does this seem like me? Or, do I have it because I was told I wanted it?" Everything was on the table.

First off, I realized I loved my kids. It's entirely possible and, I suspect, happens more often than we care to think, that people have children for reasons other than that they want them. These may seem like perfectly good reasons at the time, such as being almost thirty years old and so made aware that one is not meant to be living entirely for pleasure any longer, sleeping past 6 a.m. on Saturday mornings, owning things that break and having dinner in restaurants that don't serve up a toy with the meal.

To some extent, success in the world means having kids. This might be because the health and well-being of our economy, dressed up as success, means having kids. Or perhaps the wish to give birth is simply a biological impulse designed to ensure the continuance of our species. On particularly challenging parenting days, my sister, Keltie, and I explain our desire to have children this way, "Our hormones tricked us." I have a friend who didn't have children who claims she's going to get a T-shirt that reads, "Smarter than my hormones."

I love my kids. I wanted to be a mother. I'm grateful for that. I don't know what life would have looked like otherwise. "Someone who loves and wants these kids" went down as one of the top items on my emerging list of "Who I Am."

What did not make the list, what I realized did not make my heart sing or my soul clap its hands and exclaim, "Oh yes. This. Pursue this," were what I came to think of as "white noise" activities: listening to the radio, reading the newspaper, watching daytime television, going shopping or attending dinner parties where people talked about the newspaper, daytime television or shopping. There is nothing wrong with dinner parties, newspapers, shopping, television or people who talk about or attend them. But at that moment, I needed to connect with folk asking the same question as me. Those who might not inquire, "What do you do?" but were keen to know, "What's making you happy these days?" "What are you finding that feels like You?" These people were sent my way.

A friend I hadn't heard from in months called and mentioned a book, *The Artist's Way* by Julie Cameron. I ran out and bought a copy.

Cameron is a screenwriter and recovering alcoholic who similarly reached a stage of realizing she could no longer live as she was and...well, live. For Cameron, the confidence to express herself creatively seemed to come from a bottle. She was terrified that if she gave up alcohol, perhaps she would no longer be able to write.

Cameron needed to find a way, sober, to feel the same sense of connection to her creative impulse she found when drunk. She developed a twelve-step program, similar to AA, which not only helped her overcome her addiction and still be able to work, but which she in turn used to coach writers feeling blocked from the source of their own creative wellspring. To Cameron, and to me, this seemed like the same thing as helping people connect with their truest, most authentic Self.

Among the strategies Cameron suggests, one is to keep a daily journal. Instead of recounting the events of your day or your thoughts about life—though that can be useful and satisfying—this journal is to be random, stream of consciousness rambling. Whatever's wandering through your mind in that moment.

I began getting up a half-hour early every morning to journal. The house was quiet, the sky outside my kitchen window a soft pearly grey, the sun a thin yellow line on the horizon. I sat at the table bundled in a comforter, scratching away in a spiral notebook. As spring came on, the sun began to warm the room a little earlier each morning. I didn't need the blanket anymore. Weeks later, I would strip off my PJ top and sit in a T-shirt. I was shedding layers of my former self, stripping away years of certainty and belief, cracking open my cocoon of safety. Safety, I decided, was vastly overrated. The only place playing it safe had ever got me was sitting in a closet. I was hoping for better.

✿

I wrote six pages every morning. Whatever came into my head. In the beginning it was such erudite thoughts as, "I wish I had coffee. Why don't I have coffee? If I had gone to the store yesterday I'd be drinking coffee right now. But no, I didn't go to the store. So now? No coffee. Which really is too bad. Because I would really like to be drinking coffee."

Cameron warns not to judge what you write. She also said not to let anyone else read it. She may have suggested not even re-reading it yourself. This was welcome advice, because most of what I wrote was either coffee-related or more seeming insanity about how I was rethinking my life from the ground up.

I sorted through feelings about myself, my kids, my husband, the people I was close to and what I'd done with my life. I questioned my religion, everyone else's religion, my upbringing, my values and every decision I'd ever made. I struggled to stay open to the idea that just because a choice is hugely sensible and entirely rational, it didn't mean it was right for me.

I wrote out pain and deep desire. I wrote out joy and wonder. I wrote out confusion and puzzlement. I wrote my foolishness in having believed that by choosing the right things to put around me, I could create happiness inside. You have to work from the inside out.

I wrote out how brown my coffee cup was on the days I had coffee. I wrote about morning light filtering through new leaves on the cherry tree in my front lawn. It didn't matter what I put down. I was writing myself back to myself. Anyone can do the same thing with painting or gardening or dancing. Creating is prayer comprised entirely of listening. It's yoga for the spirit, making it both flexible and strong.

✿

To my astonishment, I was beginning to discover that at the bottom of that deep and terrifying well of loneliness what you find is only your Self. And the place that you find your Self is also where you find something even more surprising. Joy. Rampant delight. Riotous bliss. And the place you find yourself and joy and delight and bliss is also the place you find the god thing, divine connection to the universe and to our own soul. You have to. They're all the same thing. Once you've realized that, you never feel alone again.

✿

After a few weeks, I stopped getting up a half-hour early to journal. Instead, I got up an hour early. Then an hour and a half. Then two hours. By the time I was getting up two and a half hours before everyone else in our household, who rose at 7 a.m., I decided that the only way I could cope with the irrationality of getting out of bed at 4:30 a.m. to scratch in a notebook was by renaming 4:30 a.m. something that didn't sound so absurdly early. I called it "half an hour before five."

People I've told this story to say, "You must have been so disciplined." I wasn't. If anyone had suggested I get out of bed at 8 a.m. to go jogging, I would have explained that I devote that time to doing "rhythmic meditation exercises." Breathing in and out, as I sleep.

I didn't get up to write at "half an hour before five"

because I'm disciplined. I did it because I had to. I needed a couple of hours in the day just to be myself before I became what everyone else needed me to be.

✿

I would get up at half an hour before five o'clock in the morning and write until seven. Then I would start my job as a mother, wife, daughter, goddess of the household, the one responsible for turning the great wheel of my family's lives. All the time I kept asking, "Is this what I want? Is this Me?" and listening closely to the answer.

After a few more weeks, I realized that what had to be dropped from the list of "Things That Are Me/Joy/Delight/Bliss/the god thing/divine connection" was attending church. I now had full and entire faith in God. But I'd developed a serious distrust of God-wrangling. The words of our prayers and hymns emphatically insisted on the god who had failed me, the one who made life out to be a legal arrangement. I was finding that to be nonsense. For me, life was a treasure hunt. Every day I was discovering something I needed in order to be my truest, most complete Self. I was having no further dealings with that former church-wrangled-God. We'd made him so limited, belief in him could only make our lives limited in return.

What I wanted was a radical new model for my radical new understanding of the god thing, an image that spoke of the propitiousness of wolf-howling and the demise of soul-loneliness. I wanted a new name to call upon. A name that was representative of everything noble and resplendent, yet is no grander than a ladybug and no further removed than a tender breath brushing my cheek. And I wanted a picture of the divine that was mutinous, unexpected and brave. I knew where to look for such things. I would go among women. I decided to seek out some witches.

A book by Starhawk, a brilliant, thoughtful woman who is credited with reintroducing Wiccan religion to North America, had been one of the many that had recently fallen into my hands—literally. I was attempting to pull down a copy of Stendhal at the time.

Wicca, or witchcraft, is a pagan religion. This means it honours the natural world and looks to the cycles of the seasons for its symbols and lessons. Witchcraft is possibly one of our oldest religious traditions.

Being old is important in religion. In matters of religion, age is synonymous not only with respectability and often even with truth. I'm not sure why this is. Philosopher sage Ralph Waldo Emerson complained that such a stance stunts our spiritual curiosity and creativity. He suggests, "The foregoing generations beheld

God...face to face; we through their eyes. The sun shines today also... There are new lands, new men, new thoughts. Let us demand our own works and laws and worship."

✿

In other fields of life, "ancient" is more likely to infer "outdated." No scientist defends the flat earth principle on the grounds that if it was good enough to satisfy several centuries of our forefathers, it ought to be good enough for us today. In medicine, literature, communications, even in the world of fashion we progress. If this weren't the case, magazines would be full or articles insisting, "Sure, tweed gets a tad sticky in the summer but our great grandmothers wore hobble skirts in uncomfortable fabrics, so we should too." Humankind's abilities to learn and evolve are valued in every area of life except one.

In religion, antiquity often equals credibility. The older the faith tradition, the more authoritative and trustworthy we consider it to be. When you think about it, it's odd then that pagan faith paths, which clearly predate our mainstream religions, should be considered so suspect. In fact anyone trying to coax us into a return to "old-time religion," shouldn't mean reinstating prayers in Latin or embracing a moral code that was popular among passengers of the *Mayflower*. A true return to our religious roots would mean we'd all be frolicking in a dawn meadow on June twenty-first shooting fire-tipped arrows into the first rays of light, as homage to the sun god. We'd make love in haystacks under the full autumnal moon in hope that the Queen of Heaven would bless us with an abundant harvest. We'd exchange breast-shaped cakes in April to celebrate the reign of the goddess of spring. Strangely, those who favour religious traditionalism rarely advocate these sorts of activities.

The insistence on adhering to tradition even when what constitutes tradition is somewhat nonsensical and almost entirely arbitrary proved to me once again that in matters of religion, Reason was not only absent when the big decisions were on the table, it was somewhere off down the hall shooting pool with Absurdity. That was just fine. At this particular point in my life, such an arrangement suited me perfectly. If reason didn't enter into religious practice or belief, surely then I was free to go about looking for my faith path in places that I would not previously have considered quite reasonable at all.

Wicca, as described by Starhawk, is an intelligent, poetic, earth-venerating religion. The festivals and rituals are grounded in the journey of the sun, marking the passage of time in our lives by the cycles of nature.

The rituals of my church had done that too to some extent. Christmas, the birth of the son, comes at the point at which our part of the earth begins to tilt back toward the sun. "The Lord of Light" is a name given both to Christ and to the pagan sun god. Easter takes its name from Eastora, a Germanic goddess of spring. Easter celebrates Christ's resurrection as the natural world itself is reawakening. The difference is, Christian festivals are held to recount and gain inspiration from the events of the life of Christ. Wiccan holidays are designed to honour and connect with the divine spirit that reveals itself in nature. The goddess Gaia, or Mother Earth, uses the cycle of the seasons to teach us to progress gracefully through our lives and to value peace, respect and mindfulness. This emphasis on learning from nature had tremendous appeal to me. The God I now knew felt closer and more real when I was amid fens and forests than surrounded by stained-glass windows. Wicca's imagining of god as both male and female helped me begin to crack open the box in which God had been contained.

I located a local coven and was invited to join them for their winter-solstice gathering. Back in my university days, I'd met some young women calling themselves witches. They traipsed about in organic cotton smock dresses, passing out "tofu pups" and encouraging female students to "honour your vagina." At the time, I could see some justification for having them all burned at the stake.

Arriving to meet this coven, I could tell immediately that these were smart, sane women wholly committed to spiritual nurture and health. They also seemed committed to the same unbleached organic cotton clothing I recalled from my university days. Fortunately the similarities ended there.

One woman explained the Wiccan story of the solstice. The goddess is responsible for turning the wheel of the year. She makes the seasons come and go. The male god, symbolized by the sun, is the traveller through time. At the summer solstice in late June, the sun god is at the height of his potency and power. By December, increased darkness tells us that he has tired and will soon reach the conclusion of his journey. During December twenty-first and twenty-second, the forty-eight hours of the winter solstice, the god dies and is reborn. The goddess is bringer of both death and rebirth.

The message of this story is that loss, even of the most profound kind, is forever followed by new life. It is the most glorious lesson the natural world has to share. It is reassurance present in some shape and form in every religion the world has known.

In spite of having two faces, it was made clear to me that the Wiccan god and goddess are one. The distinct images are simply a means of describing how divine energy functions in the world. In a way, it sounded like a kind of cosmic dance in which god and goddess have their separate roles to play, yet are always fully connected.

I stood with other women to form a circle. The witches placed their palms on the floor, asking Mother Earth to "ground the energy" of our gathering. We joined hands and called on the spirits of the four directions, north, south, east and west, to bless us with insight, endurance, courage and compassion—the qualities needed to make a successful life passage.

We sang and chanted and then ate berries and nuts, as well as—which again concerned me a little—tofu pups. Shortly before dawn, we bundled into our coats and scarves and trooped outside to a nearby park.

Fourteen women huddled together, shivering under the trees, stamping our feet in the newly fallen snow. Then, as the first faint silvery rays of light crept over the houses and apartments at the eastern edge of the green, we clapped and shouted, joyfully greeting the return of light. Another new beginning in the endless cycle of the seasons.

✿

We headed back inside for warmth and hot chocolate, buoyed by the thought that we'd added our energy to that of the goddess as she gave birth once more. The coven leader gave us permission to take at least a little credit in the coming year for having returned the sun to the sky, ensuring that humanity continues to have life-giving heat and light. I promised myself I would do this.

It had been a beautiful night and morning. I drove home through the grey morning light I'd helped to restore to earth thinking, "Those were really great witches." It occurred to me that if anyone told me a year before I'd someday be thinking, "Those were really great witches," I would have been horrified. Instead I found myself musing how lucky I was to have been included in such an interesting, passionate group of wise women.

The solstice vigil had been inspiring. Wicca, as practised by these women, provided a compelling image of the divine and active encouragement for getting to know my own soul.

I was gradually finding communion with myself and my god thing. I now craved the kind of communion these women shared. I wanted to be part of a group of like-minded soul-seekers who understood God in the way I did. I longed to find fellow travellers with whom I could journey, studying, celebrating and sharing support along the way. Wicca would no doubt fit the bill beautifully. It just wasn't...me.

I pulled into my driveway. I needed coffee, a few hours' sleep and, after that, to keep looking. A few weeks later, I met some charming Druids.

Druidry is another earth-honouring religion that, according to legend, traces its ancestry back to the lost city of Atlantis. The story goes that the priests of Atlantis possessed special knowledge about the manipulation of natural energy. Some of these leaders used their privileged position to satisfy their greed and personal lust for power. The result was widespread suffering and eventually, the total destruction of the city. Picture the stock market crash of 2008, with all the investment brokers wearing togas. It was kind of like that.

Among the priests who managed to escape the burning ruins of Atlantis were those who believed that their secrets and wisdom were to be used to live in balance and respect with nature. They travelled to many parts of the world, some settling at last in the Celtic regions of Ireland and Britain. These are the Druids who are thought to have built Stonehenge, considered a feat of mathematical genius that supposedly served as a calendar for these ancient wisemen. Personally, I've never been that overawed by this particular achievement. "There's snow on the rocks. Must be winter." Very impressive.

Druids are considered to have been influential in Celtic culture both as religious sages and medical healers. They were sought after to teach the sons of noblemen and kings. Some were elevated to kingship themselves. But, as Christianity began to push itself onto the people of the Celtic regions, the Druids, like all who practised nature-centred religions, were either slaughtered or joined the more scholarly Christian monastic orders.

Like Wicca, Druidism has experienced a resurgence in the past few decades in spite of public parks now having ordinances against strapping virgins to oak trees, painting them blue and ritually sacrificing them. At least I think it's implied in most park permits.

For me, the appeal of Druidism was its aura of mysticism and enchantment. Individual groups are called "groves," which conjures up images of wood nymphs and magical hidden glades. Groves produces thrills. My former faith tradition had congregations. I couldn't recall congregations having ever produced any thrills whatsoever.

The grove I managed to track down was made up of two smart, thoughtful twenty-year-old men who were very keen on reclaiming the use of swords in religious ceremony. They choose Druidism as their religious path for its connection to nature and to mystery; they found immediacy and illumination in the ancient words and rituals, a fire and magic they hadn't experienced in the Christianity they'd been brought up with.

I attended several grove gatherings, our group comprised of these two young men and me, with the occasional addition of one young man's girlfriend—a sprightly nineteen year old who had to leave early to get to her job as a nightclub go-go dancer. Our study sessions wound up at about 11 p.m., after which my fellow Druids would head out for a night of clubbing and I would go home to bed.

Each week as I drove to our meeting, I would wonder, "Is this the path for me?" I liked these young Druids. I was awed by the fearlessness they brought to the daunting business of knowing their own soul. And that they managed this at an age when I'd thought it the height of religious courage to flout the rules and go to a Sunday movie matinee. I was touched by their complete willingness to welcome into their midst a woman old enough to be their...well, quite young mother. And I was moved by the fine words and heroic imagery of the Druid rituals. I didn't necessarily want to wield a sword while I worshipped, but so far this hadn't been required.

Once again, I'd found a bright, sincere group of fellow followers after the god thing. Once again, I finally had to admit that this just wasn't the faith path for me.

✿

After bowing out of the grove, I spent an evening with people who spoke in animal voices, channelling the divine within. With another group, I knelt in a hayfield, calling on the blessing of the moon, while scattering hard beans over my shoulder to encourage fertile growth of the spirit. I went anywhere a group of god-and-soul-seekers gathered, prepared to try, at least once, whatever others had found that stirred their spirit. Sometimes, the rituals I took part in seemed downright silly. But I reminded myself that the traditions of my church were not all entirely sensible. Sometimes, the words and images shared were arresting and beautiful. Often, I felt clearly the deep need among the participants, an intense and painful longing to connect with the god-thing inside and beyond themselves. I knew this need. I honoured them for it.

Finally, after an evening of voodoo drumming followed by a vegan potluck where I ate soy in more forms than I would have thought possible, I was driving home once again. Suddenly, I was struck by an astonishing thought: "What was wrong with the God I knew?"

Well, not quite the one I knew. But maybe a slightly revised version.

I was through with that "faith as a legal agreement" nonsense, of course. I was not going back to the "blind obedience = happiness" model. The god who decreed those things was like Zeus or Odin, lost in the mists of time, banished from the landscape of my psyche forever. But perhaps, in turning away so entirely from the image of the god I'd grown up with, I'd thrown out the baby with the sacramental water. It was worth considering. I'd learned to see through God-wrangling and religious doctrine that made the divine sound petty or foolish. Maybe that cleared the way to knowing god in a whole new light.

✿

I decided I was ready to take a stab at forging a fresh relationship with the god of the Bible. I would once again enter into community with those who found spiritual nurture and inspiration in the stories of Genesis and Exodus. But I wasn't going back to church. Instead, I headed to a local synagogue. I would take classes for conversion to Judaism.

Judaism is another ancient religion though not so old as paganism. The age difference is easy to detect. Pagan holidays centre on themes of hunting and gathering, emphasizing men and women living as equals with the rest of creation and in communion with nature. Jewish festivals emerged in a later period. Humans were still tied to the earth but now favoured farming as a means of feeding their growing tribes. Judaism's sacred observances reflect mankind's increasing mastery over the natural world. There is still a connection to the cycles of the seasons, but the focus is on human action, planting and harvesting, rather than the gracious free-will generosity of the earth.

Traces of its pagan origins can still be found in modern Judaism, just as they are in Christianity. The monthly observance of *Rosh Hodesh*, for example, marks the advent of the new moon. In some places, this point in the lunar cycle is celebrated with a festive meal and the lighting of candles. Jewish feminists have embraced *Rosh Hodesh* as a time for women to gather together to honour the affinity between their bodies and the phases of the moon.

I found a rabbi prepared to sponsor me and began the process of becoming Jewish. I arrived at the shul for the inaugural class, breathless with excitement, confident that in this rich and venerable faith path, I would find not only a vision of the divine I could embrace but also the community for study, observance and encouragement I longed for.

The first thing I learned in my course was that most people converting to Judaism are not "plucky but disillusioned former Christians who have appreciated but not ultimately bonded with paths of paganism." You'd think they would be, but they're not. Every other person in my class, except one, was a pert young blond woman of no particular religious persuasion who wanted to marry her Jewish fiancé and have his parents' blessing when they did it.

I had no problem with this. These women were determined learners, able to explain the importance of *halakhah*, rattle off the symbolism of *matzah* or describe the proper care and storage of a prayer scroll faster than the rabbi could say, "Perhaps you'd like to field this question, Tiffany."

Besides me, the only other non-engaged gentile in our group was a man in his mid-thirties, Graham, who had recently found out he'd been adopted. All Graham knew about his birth mother was that she was Jewish. We quickly became friends, sitting side by side each week, trading study notes and support.

The rabbi assigned to teach us was a tiny, energetic man who practised and shared his faith with passion. He hopped about the room, beard flying, eyes twinkling, pronouncing gleefully, "Of course we stand up for the *Amidah* prayer. It is too beautiful. Who could stay sitting down?" Or, "Do not complain about keeping the Sabbath. To rest is a gift. Do you argue with a gift? What's a gift about going to the mall?"

Our rabbi taught us that "Israel" means "wrestles with God." The name reminds us that faith isn't something we're supposed to accept without question. Understanding the divine and our relationship to it is a lifelong process that's meant to involve questioning, struggling and praying for guidance. When studying scripture, he insisted, the aim should never be to arrive at one definitive interpretation. Our challenge is to discover how many different meanings there might be, even in a single word or sentence, then to sort through them to determine what seems like truth to us in that moment or, better still, what stretches our understanding of what is loving and just. Every phrase, every story can offer a variety of ways to know god and the means by which we may live well and gently together in the world.

Besides the importance of study, the rabbi also insisted on the significance of home. He said we should know where we come from and have respect for our past. He noted that sometimes we're called to change the faith tradition we inherit, but that for the most part, if you can, it's best to stay with the religion you were born into. There may be a reason for you to be there.

One evening as my classmates and I were packing up our prayer books and Hebrew dictionaries and filing out—the engaged couples chattering, swapping recommendations of kosher caterers and where to purchase an impressive *ketubah*, Graham dogging after them, passing out fliers for an upcoming lecture on modern Zionism—the rabbi pulled me aside. He asked which among my classmates I felt I had the most in common with. I answered, "Graham. Because he's just here for himself, not for someone else." Then, the rabbi asked what I thought the difference between Graham and I was. I found myself saying, "Graham's trying to find his roots. I'm running away from mine."

Graham went on to convert to Judaism and to take a leadership role in that community. I went home.

It wasn't easy to return to Christianity and the Church. Going back felt a little like returning to a battle zone after the war is finally over. It was impossible not to grieve the world that was, the one that hadn't provided answers but had offered a kind of sleepy reassurance nonetheless. Before me was the struggle to see what, if anything, was left amid the rubble of my disappointment and disillusionment that could be grown or forged into a new faith, what could be salvaged, what must be replaced. The god of contracts was blown to bits, of course. Gradually, fresh images and ideas began to poke themselves out of newly cleared ground. Tiny flowers of insight and slips of inspiration emerged—green, potent and scented like spring.

My studies in Judaism had taught me the importance of study. Without much enthusiasm, I enrolled as a part-time student at my church's seminary college, a place teeming with exuberant Christians embracing a call to become ordained pastors.

I arrived for my first class and heaved open the college's massive wooden front doors thinking they were the very symbols of enduring God-wrangling; fortress walls, weighty oppressive barricades of "non-listening" designed to keep God contained. I vowed silently, "I will study at this place...but no way am I ever becoming a minister."

✿

Throughout this time, as I searched for a faith path, I was still getting up at half an hour before five to scribble in my notebook. One day I suddenly left off writing about the concerns of my little life and soul or the colour of my coffee mug. Instead, I found myself writing a story about a young woman who was not me. In the weeks that followed, I sprang out of bed each morning in the pre-dawn, eager to read the next installment of this person's adventure as my hand and pen wrote it out.

After several months, I came to a shocking realization. I was writing a novel. I told myself this was ridiculous. Sure, I had already participated in many activities lately that might be considered absurd, such as dancing in circles with a group of women I'd barely met in order to raise a "cone of power," or debating the mystical, sacred nature of trees or finally imagining that I, cover girl for *WASP Monthly*, might be destined to uncover her inner Jew. I was willing to admit that some people, particularly those closest to me, had found these activities a trifle offbeat. Writing a novel, however, was grounds to have me committed.

The world does not require more novels. In fact it doesn't even need a good many of the ones it has now. Anything by Kingsley Amis, for example, could be dispensed with without our feeling the loss one bit. Abolish all historical romance that doesn't have Georgette Heyer's name on the cover and a visit to the library shelves would still be as satisfying as ever.

Also, no one gets a first novel published. This may in fact be the only completely universal truth. Everyone knows it. Everyone accepts it. Given this, how any books exist at all is something of a mystery.

By the time I had six hundred handwritten pages it was hard to avoid the idea that I was, indeed, writing a novel. I decided to deal with this the same way I'd coped with getting up half an hour before five. I would rename the event into something that sounded rational. Or as close to rational as I could manage. In the case of writing a novel, I would call it "journaling about someone else's life."

All during these months, I continued to look at every choice I'd made, asking, "Is this what I want?" My husband, Michael, was doing the same. We went together to couples' counselling, but what quickly became clear was that, for both of us, these were exit interviews. Our marriage ended. Together and apart we began the difficult task of learning what our lives looked like now.

One cool, breezy October evening, I trudged over to my church for a meeting. Our minister was doing her PhD thesis on Old Testament interpretation and she'd asked me to sit on a committee that would meet regularly to discuss her research. The group comprised members of our congregation and a few folk from a neighbouring church.

I was the first to arrive. I took off my jacket, slung it over the back of a chair and sat down at the big board table in the empty meeting room to wait. After ten minutes, the door opened. A woman I had never met walked in. I took one look at her. And I thought, "Oh, my god. I'm gay."

There is an old joke about a man who arrives late for an important appointment and finds the parking lot of the building entirely full. He drives up and down the lines of parked cars thinking, "Please God, give me a parking space. I'll go to church next Sunday. I'll go to church every Sunday. I'll go to church every Sunday, I'll join the choir and I'll double my givings." Suddenly, he spots an empty space right at the door of the building. He pulls his car in, turns off the ignition and prays, "Never mind, I found one."

I had prayed, asked, begged for an answer to, "What is Me? Who am I?" God had responded in spades. Now I didn't want to pay the price. Which was, ironically, getting what I wanted.

I didn't want to be gay. This wasn't because I had a problem with people who were gay. In my years of running a theatre company I'd employed and been friendly with many gay people. I just didn't want to be gay myself.

I couldn't be lesbian. It was out of the question. I lived in the most suburban part of my city. I carpooled my kids to soccer practice and art class. I didn't have the cheekbones for a short hair cut. And I was never, ever, going to join a softball league.

I certainly didn't want my children to have to deal with what their friends might say about them having a lesbian mother. I'd already disturbed our lives with a divorce. And, I'd disturbed my own by almost becoming Wiccan, Druid, Jewish, going back to school and putting in hours a day writing my "journal about someone else's life." I'd ventured plenty close enough to the margins of what was reasonable and acceptable, thank you very much. I couldn't do this as well. If "gay" was part of the answer to who I was, then I didn't want to know.

I struggled. I bargained ("Let me be half of who I really am and still be entirely happy..."). I railed. I cried. Often. This was more frightening than the wolf-howling. That would stop, one way or the other. This was who I was for good.

In the weeks that followed, I maintained a running dialogue in my mind that went something like this:

ME: "This is not what I signed on for."

THE GOD THING: "What did you sign on for?"

ME: "To find what feeds my soul."

GT: "This would be it."

ME: "It's not what I was expecting."

GT: "Ah, that's a different issue altogether."

Or,

ME: "I'm having real trouble seeing how this can be for the best."

GT: "I suppose that's why I'm God and you're not."

In all the sage and august wisdom literature that describes God as good, loving, transcendent, I can't believe that no one thought to mention that God may also be smug.

I admitted what I was feeling to my ex-husband, Michael, who asked, "So, what are you really afraid of?"

I answered, "I'm afraid of being isolated. Alone. Shut out from what I really want."

He said, "Maybe accepting that you're gay is the way for you not to be."

It's in those moments, when you suddenly glimpse the brave new world God has in store for you and perhaps find it's hard to distinguish it from your worst nightmare, that there is one decision and one decision alone to be made. You're in or you're out. That's it. You're in or you're out. There are no half commitments in a spiritual life. There are no caveats and no conditions. The option to say, "I'll listen as long as I am totally comfortable with what I hear," does not exist. If that's your stance, you may never hear anything at all.

With the god thing, it's all or nothing. This is the way of true love. You're in or you're out.

I thought long and hard about what life had been like before knowing my Self and the god thing. I decided I was in.

So, I blessed the universe that created this funny old world where anything can happen including the point at which Michael and I stopped being married being the moment we began a real relationship. And, where a city-suburban-soccer-mom who will never pull off a crop cut, realizes she's lesbian and then must prepare herself to see this as a good thing.

In the years since, I've heard numerous stories from gay men and women who have had this same, striking flash of realization about their sexual preference. Comedian Rosie O'Donnell said she was driving her car one day and suddenly thought, "Hey...I'm gay." Personally, I'm glad I was not operating heavy machinery at the time.

I screwed up my courage and asked out the woman from my church committee. We dated for two years. The sky didn't fall. My kids didn't trade their soccer games and art classes for hard drugs and facial tattoos. Later, when I met my partner, Liz, and we eventually began living together, she was welcomed onto the street by my neighbours. We were married in my church with our families not simply present, but cheering us on.

On our wedding day, waiting for the ceremony to start, I spent a quiet moment reflecting on the past few years. If there has been anything predictable about my faith journey it has been the element of surprise. I've never known what was coming next. Contract or no contract, the god thing does a terrible job of keeping us safe. But it has an unparalleled knack for making life interesting.

This day was no exception. After years of declaring I would never marry again, I joyfully and gratefully took hold of Liz's hand and we walked down the aisle into our future together.

Before that, I had finished the novel and found a publisher. And I had announced to my college registrar that I would like to leave the study stream designed for students with a general interest in theology and enroll in the one specific to those training for ordained church ministry. I thought, perhaps when others are struggling to hear or to keep from hearing, "Who are you?" I could be there with encouragement and support. A friend along the way.

✿

Someone once suggested, "If God wanted to get your attention, what would God do?" The answer? "*Think* at you!" Obviously, I needed a little more help than that. God thought at me and I put on the radio or the television. God thought harder and I picked up a book. Or, I worried. I went shopping. I planned. "La, la, la," I covered my ears, "I don't hear you. Ho no, boy. Not me. La, la, la." Finally, God had simply said aloud, "You. Now." And nothing was ever the same.

Growing up, I think anyone in my church family would have said that a person who believes God has spoken to them has lost their mind. But that's OK by me. By losing my mind, I healed my heart. By letting go of the person I thought I should be, I discovered the person I always was. And, by losing faith in everything I believed I wanted, I found greater fulfillment than I could have imagined possible.

A few weeks ago, I drove north out of our city to an Aboriginal healing centre near Midland, Ontario. My course to become a minister included a chance to study another ancient faith path, Native Canadian spirituality taught by Aboriginal elders. As the final event, our class was invited to participate in a sweat lodge, a deeply sacred ritual of physical and spiritual healing.

I was more than a little nervous about this. The heat

in these lodges is extreme, intended to burn wisdom onto the heart as it detoxifies the body. Some people can't bear it. And among those who manage to stick it out, some experience startling visions. One man had told me he'd seen an eagle sweep over his head and been terrified. I pulled into the parking lot of the centre, already starting to sweat a little. I'd been through a few intense spiritual experiences in my life. I knew enough to be scared.

Dingy patches of snow swaddled puddles of mud along the pock-marked laneway, signs of spring not quite arrived. The scent of pine and cedar was pungent in the crisp afternoon air.

I followed my classmates to a utilitarian meeting building. The inside walls were decorated with posters of howling wolves. I found this familiar. Even comforting. The windows sparkled with dream catchers, glittering webs of twigs, feathers and beads.

For two hours, our small group of men and women, non-Native and Christian, listened to an elder teach the story of the sweat lodge, interweaving ancient myth and lore with practical instruction, preparing both our minds and spirits for communion with the celestial guides.

There are some prohibitions against women using the lodge. Menstruating women are not allowed inside. Our teacher explained that this is not because they are considered weak or unclean. Quite the reverse is true. This is a time of great strength for females. "During the period of sloughing off and renewal," he said, "women hold a powerful energy inside them. I was trying to start a fire once and next to me was standing a woman who was menstruating. Her energy was so strong I couldn't get the match to light. That's why a woman shouldn't go into the lodge at those times. The strength of her spirit could be overwhelming to those around her."

Pregnant women do not go in either. "The lodge is for rebirth," the elder explained. "A woman carrying a baby already has new life inside. What more could be given to her?" Also, while it's believed that children choose the family they will be born to, he noted, "Before a spirit has a body, if the expecting mother goes into the lodge and takes that unborn soul among the spirits of the elders, it might decide it would rather go back with them instead of coming into this world. We don't want that to happen. So women carrying unborn babies don't go into the lodge."

People who drank heavily the night before don't participate either. "The spirits have to make the sweat so hot to purify you," our teacher said. "It becomes too intense for everyone else."

We learned that the lodge was given as a gift to the Native people for healing and inner strength. "I did a lot of hard work there," our elder told us, "when I was giving up drinking. I sweated out a lot of bad thoughts there. The spirits took them away."

We were shown which direction to go to enter the lodge. The entry pathway traces the course of the sun. Stepping across the line running between the lodge and the sacred fire outside must be avoided. It cuts the connection with the sun's power.

When the teaching was done, the men of our group went outside to prepare a fire that would heat the sacred stones. The women were sent to collect snippets of cedar boughs. We were instructed to place a pinch of tobacco at the base of each tree, ask the tree spirit for permission to take a frond, listen for a reply, and then to pinch off an end, gently, with our fingertips.

In late April, the air was damp and frosty. By the time we reached the cedar hedges, the sun was already vanishing from the hazy grey sky.

After an hour of pinching, our fingers were numb, but we chatted and laughed together. Someone noted that the men seemed to be simply hanging around the fire while the women got ready everything necessary. We decided this proves all cultures are basically alike.

As darkness fell, we hauled the cedar clippings back to the meeting hall in a large sack. An elder took them away to strew the fronds on the floor of the sweat lodge. The men changed into swimming trunks, the women into cotton sundresses and we all headed back outside, down the dirt road to where a fire was blazing.

The sweat lodge was a low, unadorned, tentlike structure. An arched frame of sapling boughs had been bound together with twine and covered over with blue plastic tarps. The floor was dried mud covered with more tarps and a few grey woollen blankets and finished with a layer of the fragrant cedar fronds.

The entire structure was not more than four feet high in the centre and twelve feet across. Inside, a deep pit had been dug into the ground in the middle. This is where the white-hot stones would be placed. Splashing water onto these igneous rocks creates the steam.

We entered the lodge on our hands and knees. There certainly wasn't room to stand. One by one, we paused at the threshold, repeated a Native greeting to the spirits, said our name and then crawled inside, taking a place around the pit.

When everyone was in, we were pushed close together, to sit on cold hard ground, our noses full of the clean scent of cedar and our legs outstretched, toes toward the fire pit. Five stones were carried in on shovels. We greeted each new arrival with a shout of joy. The rocks are the spirit ancestors, come to bring us wisdom and healing. They must be welcomed with respect into the circle. One member of our class was instructed to lean over the pit and toss in offerings of cedar tips as the elder recited a Native prayer.

When all the stones were in place, the outside flap was closed. Blackness. Cold. Then, the sharp rasp of frigid water meeting hot stone. In that low, confined space, we were quickly enveloped in vapour.

From hand to hand, wet shoulders pressed tightly against each other, we passed around a small drum. As each person received the drum, they were to strike it three times. Then, say their name again. It's important in Native healing to say your name, important to know and to claim who you are. Next, we were to offer a prayer for someone else, followed by one for ourselves. Finally, we were to say what healing we had come to receive. "You should know why you've come here," our leader advised. "That goes for the lodge and for your life."

The thickening steam was intense and oppressive. Some members of our group found themselves struggling for breath and asked to leave. As the flap was opened a shock wave of icy air pierced the darkness and heat, yanking us back into the world outside.

The flap dropped back into place. We were cocooned with the spirits once more.

A few newly heated rocks had been added to the pit. Droplets of water sizzled and danced across the fiery surfaces. The cedar tip offerings flared like tiny fireworks as they hit white stone.

Sweat gushed down my limbs like rivers in springtime. Salty rivulets dripped from my forehead onto my eyelids and lips. My cotton dress was soon drenched entirely, plastered against my soaking thighs and back. My hair clung to my neck and forehead. I could feel the perspiring bodies of my classmates pressed tightly against me on either side.

In the blackness, someone's hand found mine, closing my fingers around the drum. I beat it three times. I said my name. Then a prayer for my children, that each find her path in life and, if the spirits would be so kind and willing, that their journey not be quite so perplexing as mine had been. I said a prayer for myself, that I be able to walk my path with courage even when the road ahead doesn't seem clear.

Now, I was to ask for what I needed to know. I had intended to ask what I was meant to do next in my life. I was at the point of having to make a definite commitment if I wanted to become an ordained minister. I had significant doubts about following this course, doubts about taking on a job that would surely require more than I had to give. I was already doing that as a parent, as a partner and as a person trying to live a mindful, spiritual existence. I wasn't sure I wanted anything more added to my list.

I opened my mouth to speak the question I had prepared, "What is my way?" Instead, I found myself asking, "Where is my joy?"

The unexpected. God cannot be contained. Not even in our own plan of what we're going to say in a sweat lodge.

Then, amid the warm press of bodies and prayer-charged air, the voice that had spoken clearly and tenderly so many years ago when my soul howled in need, now said just as audibly, and just to me, "It's here."

Martin Buber was a modern-day Jewish philosopher. He said many stupendously smart and insightful things. What he said was so smart and so insightful that Buber's writings ought to come with a warning label. Something like, "Contents of this book may cause brain to explode."

Straight up, Buber is safe only in very, very small doses. In fact, no one should ever read Buber. Buber is complex. Buber is dense. Buber is labyrinthine. Buber actually uses words such as "labyrinthine," which shows you just how complex, dense and labyrinthine he really is.

What you might want to do is read someone else explaining Buber to you. This is a similar principle to viewing an eclipse of the sun by looking at a reflected image. Or, it being safe to visit places after the Virgin Mary or Christ has appeared there, but not to attempt to make actual contact yourself. In an unfiltered state, these events are too much for us. But seen from a distance you're able to get a sense of the thing without risking having your brain turned into a Jello-whirlpool-imploding-supernova.

What I offer here is a tiny sampling of Buber. This is "Buber-lite."

Martin Buber said, "There is something that can be found in one place. It is a great treasure, which may be called the fulfillment of existence. The place where this treasure can be found is the place on which one stands."

Even from those few lines, we feel our minds explode just a little. What we most desire, the answer to "Who am I?" and the sense of true belonging and enduring communion, isn't something to be searched for. You won't find it in a shopping mall or analyst's office or even in the right relationship or by choosing a perfect faith path. It isn't anything that we're required to purchase, pursue or achieve.

What we need to fulfill our deepest longing, we already have. It's inside us. Every one of us. Right now. It was inside me all along. All I had to do was listen.

When it was time to crawl out from of the damp shelter of the sweat lodge, we were invited to leave behind us any thought or behaviour that did not nurture our soul. The elder told us to simply toss it away. Let it be burned up in the pit by the sacred fire. Then, we were to raise ourselves up as we passed back through the doorway. Let out a cry. Send a yowl of new life into the cold night air.

I pulled myself through the open flap, looked up at the first bright stars of evening and I howled for all I was worth. A great, deep cry of joy. Then I went to stand beside my classmates, gathering around a campfire, to give thanks.

II
Losing Ground

...in Which My Child Becomes Transgendered and I Become Transformed

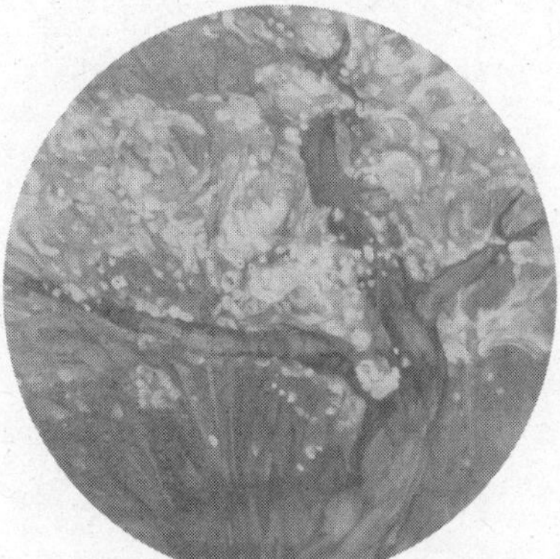

On the third Thursday evening of every month, I make my way downtown to a typical high-rise office building, take the elevator to the third floor and go down the hallway to a very commonplace meeting room. By the time I arrive, the room is usually filled with twenty or thirty middle-aged, middle-class people like myself. As ordinary-looking a group of adults as you could find. We greet each other, introduce ourselves to newcomers, sip bottled water and chat about the weather, work, politics and pets.

At 7 p.m., we take seats around a boardroom table. And, for the next two hours, discussion is animated, occasionally raucous and often tearful as we share opinions about what plastic surgeon makes the best surgically constructed penis or whether it's a father's responsibility to take his son to buy a bra. The group is "Transceptance." This is my support circle for parents of transgendered* children.

*I have used "transgendered" to describe my child throughout this essay because it is the one most commonly used. However "transsexual" is a more technically accurate label. A transsexual is a person whose inner knowledge of themself as male or female does not correspond to their biological sex. A transgendered person is simply someone who does not conform to their society's norms for masculine/feminine.

Four years ago, I didn't lose a son, I...no, I did. I lost a son. Other members of Transceptance lost daughters. Our children didn't go anywhere, they just became honest about who they really are. Sons "came out" as daughters. Daughters "came out" as sons. And their parents became members of this support group.

Some of our conversations are about the effects of hormone therapy or where to buy a "Jane belt." But often, we use this time to talk out our fears and disappointment, our anger and our hope. We cry a lot. We laugh just as often. We hug each other. Together, we try to learn what our children's transitions are teaching us. The one thing we are all put on the earth to learn: We are learning how to love.

Transceptance meetings begin by each member telling their story. Mine could be organized into chapters with titles such as, "My Child Is Unhappy," "My Child Comes Out," "I Melt Down," "My Child Begins to Be Happier," "I Calm Down," "My Child Has Gender-Reassignment Surgery," "I Lose It Again," "My Child Is Much, Much Happier," "I Calm Down Again"...the rest is still to be written.

The story of my eldest child, Jade, is not only about how Jade's life changed. It's about how mine became different as well. It's also about how her father's life was altered, and how her younger sister, Becky, was affected. It's about how her grandmother adapted, how her uncles and aunts adjusted and how her cousins coped. It's a fact of family life that when one member of the group changes, the others must change too. The end result is as individual as we are.

Jade's experience is also about how the life and worldview of her high school guidance counsellor was altered, along with those of her principal and her fellow students. Our city newspaper ran an article on Jade: "Local high school student-council president transgenders." The article changed the lives of people I'd never met, including several who later joined my Transceptance group, reporting that their child had come out to them clutching a copy of Jade's story.

The tale of Jade's transformation is one each person it touched would tell a little differently. This is my version. For me, the story begins with family.

We all know that the purpose of family is to provide us with the affection and sense of belonging we all require. Our parents and siblings are those who love us entirely, not for anything we've done, but simply because we exist. They are living, breathing covered wagons of emotional support and nurture, circling around to protect us when the forces of life threaten our well-being and our self-esteem. Family provides a soft, safe place to be in a hard and dangerous world. This is the purpose of family.

Until a very few years ago, I would have said this was true. But then, a few years ago I also would have said that having a vagina made a person female or having a penis made a person male. As my friend Avi would say, "What I didn't know was a lot."

Most family differences, and I include those of my own family here, stem from this much cherished, profoundly embedded belief that the role of family members is to provide us with a sense of being loved and accepted, a feeling that we're standing on solid ground. Given the experience of the last five years I would, in fact, contend that this is, to use the most technically correct term "a load of hooey." In fact, the main and most important role of those closest to you is to yank your metaphorical chain, poke you with a psychic stick, bring up your most deep-rooted, vexing personal issues and make you totally insane. The definition of family is not "people who push one another's buttons." It's "people who push one another's buttons, hold them down and then slap a piece of duct tape over them."

✿

I once heard a statistic that 82 per cent of all family groups display one or more traits that would classify them as "dysfunctional." This seems pretty far off the mark to me. I'd put it at 100 per cent. "I love my family but they make me crazy," is one of the most commonly heard phrases in the world. "Honour your father and mother" is no doubt included in the Ten Commandments because it's recognized that not killing your parents is sometimes only possible with legislation.

There are exceptions, of course. My older sister, Keltie, does not make me crazy. She makes me better. Keltie and I were born two years apart. We grew up alternately screaming at each other or, on a good day, ignoring each other altogether. When we became adults, we were suddenly best friends. I don't know how this happened. Perhaps it's a typical result of becoming reasonable and mature. Or, it's a typical result of becoming wise enough to realize you can't make it in life alone.

The best thing Keltie does is help me blow off a little emotional steam now and then. We do this by participating in what we call *Anne and Keltie Moments*. An *Anne and Keltie Moment* is a short, designated space of time during which Keltie and I can say anything we want about another person but—and this is the brilliant part—at the end we still get to qualify as being nice people.

Whatever is said during an *Anne and Keltie Moment* remains strictly between the two of us. It does not, and this is very important, seep into the outside world, thus potentially causing bad energy or giving us negative karma. It's as if, just for that space of time, we're circumventing the natural order of the universe. We're almost sure this is possible.

A typical *Anne and Keltie Moment* goes something like this.

ME: "That woman we met seemed very pleasant. Don't you think she was pleasant?"

KELTIE: "Pleasant. Yes."

ME: "Yes."

KELTIE: "Pleasant."

(Pause)

ME: "Can we have an *Anne and Keltie Moment*?"

KELTIE: "Oh my god, yes."

ME: "The woman's a total witch."

KELTIE: "Witch is being kind."

You get the idea.

Anne and Keltie Moments are useful because occasionally, just now and then, you know...rarely...on an extremely limited basis, of course, the person we wish to discuss is among those we love best in the world. There are five adult children in our family, all outgoing, independent, strong-minded people. So, naturally we make each other nuts.

When the chips are down, if one of us is getting divorced or loses a job or there's a family emergency, everyone rallies round and supports each other, no question. Which is what really matters. But on a day-to-day basis, as most people do with those they love, we bicker, we squabble, we pick at each other's psychic scabs, we have difficulty seeing life from the other's perspective.

There is a reason for this. The universe is determined

that, no matter how much we dig in our emotional heels, pound our psychological fists, refuse, ignore, demur or decline the offer, we're going to learn to be better people. To ensure this happens, it arranges for us to be placed in these groups called "families." Rather than being cocoons of devotion and belonging, families are roiling scrums of fellow learners. Each of us has been meticulously selected and purposefully placed together for the sole and express purpose of bringing each other's deepest, thorniest emotional issues into the full light of day. Our job is to illuminate for each other the most gaping, glaring places in our individual personal makeup where we could stand the most improvement.

Needless to say, we do not like this. Which is why the job has to be done by people you are biologically chained to, those you can never truly escape regardless of time, distance or the benefits of call display.

✿

Among the many emotional issues my family kindly illuminates for me is one I call my "nut button." A nut button is a tender or bruised spot on the psyche that is eternally tender to the touch. It's that one topic or opinion another person may bring up that's guaranteed to send you into a tailspin, reducing you to an infantile, shrieking frenzy, usually just at a point when you're congratulating yourself on having become mature and self-composed. Simply put, a nut button is the personal issue that always and inevitably makes you nuts.

My nut button is the belief that people think I'm irresponsible or, as I usually phrase it when complaining to myself, that they don't take me seriously. In hindsight, becoming a humour writer may not have been the best way of counteracting this feeling. This seems proof, in fact, that the Fates enjoy a good laugh.

✿

In order to ensure that this issue—"Others do not take me seriously"—remains at the front and centre of my psyche at all times, the powers that be placed me with parents and siblings who have professions such as teacher, lawyer, banker, social worker and turf care expert. My family members are logical, reasonable, rational people, every one of them. And, in their logical, reasonable, rational way, they have always known exactly what to make of a lateral-thinking, impulsive, artsy, "I'm following my inner voice even if its GPS appears to be on the blink" type person such as myself. They think I'm flighty. "Anne is flighty" is a generally held truth among my closest relatives. They believe it.

And I believe it too.

As an adult, I have done many things to disprove this statement. I've earned a university degree, held down responsible jobs, headed a company, managed a household, raised children, juggled not only my own diverse needs and desires but those of everyone around me, all with some reasonable amount of competency (i.e., No one died. Or got left behind at soccer practice.). In spite of this, I remain convinced that I am flighty. I assume that no one will take me seriously.

Nut buttons have nothing to do with reality. They're immune to fact or example. So, on past occasions when I did something that was sensible, solid and responsible, it never occurred to me that this contradicted my view of myself. If, however, I did something that could be characterized as flighty, I sucked this in and pinned it prominently onto the bulletin board of my psyche as proof of my innate and abiding flightiness. Proof that my family was right.

Everyone has at least one nut button. Almost everyone. The only person I have ever met who has no spiritual tumour, no oozing knot of self-not-loving that the universe is just itching to bring into the open, is my partner, Liz. I spent the first six months of our relationship struggling to figure out what Liz's issues might be. Finally, I realized she doesn't have any. The only possible response to this was to marry her. Because, fortunately, I have enough for two. Other than Liz though, I question whether there is a person walking the face of the earth that doesn't have many major emotional issues.

✿

When attempting to identify your own nut button, there are two fail-proof methods to choose from. You can dedicate yourself to a multiyear course of intensive, mentally gruelling "down in the trenches of the soul" analysis by a licensed professional therapist. Or, you may choose a more direct but much more difficult, emotionally perilous route. You can attend a family gathering.

Among family, the issue of how you see yourself, something you will have learned as a child, is always easy to spot. This is because among family, no one ever progresses past the emotional age of seven years old.

No matter how long I live, no matter how mature, refined or enlightened I may become, my brother Bruce has only to say, "Remember the time Anne set fire to the dining-room table?" (Or "Remember the time Anne tried to change her name to Venus Aphrodite?" Or "The time Anne tried to drive north out of Toronto and ended up at Lake Ontario?"...) and I become a yowling prepubescent child again.

It doesn't matter that Bruce slaved over an organ adaptation of "Hockey Night in Canada" to play at Liz and my wedding, in honour of Liz's love of the game. It doesn't matter that Bruce phones me when I have a book published to say how proud he is of me. It doesn't matter that in the case of any emergency I know for certain that Bruce will step up to the plate with kindness and openhearted support. In other words, it doesn't matter that I know that Bruce loves and values me. At that moment, all I hear is whatever Bruce has said or done that feeds my belief that I am flighty and no one takes me seriously.

It is at those moments, when we feel our most stinging issues being set off like heat-seeking missiles aimed straight at our self-esteem, that there is a choice to be made. Not a choice as to whether or not we'll become yowling prepubescent children. That's going to happen. The choice I have in such a situation is this. I can tell myself (and any sibling who'll listen) that Bruce is a jerk, he's acting like a total infant and he'd better stop it or I'm going to tell our mother on him. And truthfully, this is usually what I do. But another option would be to remind myself that my brother has, in fact, provided a very useful service. He has shown me the places where I'm in need of a little personal development. He has identified the key to achieving inner peace by reminding me of the importance of believing that I am loved and valued. He has given me a precious opportunity to choose to trust that belief and preserve my sense of well-being. And for all that, I should thank him.

Being grateful to the people who help you see your nut buttons, and this sometimes includes not just family but co-workers, friends, perhaps even the person standing in front of you in the line clearly marked "eight items only" who obviously has ten, is not easy. What's easy is being left with the feeling that in the grand stadium of life, the gods are continually tossing us into the arena with exactly whichever lions are likely to cause the most grief. We duck and weave, struggling to lift our tender egos out of reach of flying claws and pointy teeth. It's difficult to recall, "Ah yes, I must thank these lions. They are here to show me the places I need to learn to love myself more. They are here to teach me." Mostly, we don't want to be taught. The universe has a strategy to deal with this as well. It sends bigger lions.

Being able to recognize our nut buttons, the way our self-not-loving manifests itself in our life, is essential to achieving health and happiness. It determines not only how content we are in ourselves but also how content we're able to be in our relationships. Which is important. Because human beings, no matter how much we like to think of ourselves as independent and self-sufficient, are hardwired for relationships.

This brings to mind an old party game, which was to ask, "If you could have all the money you wanted but never have any close relationships or anyone to share it with, would you choose that?" It would be hard to imagine any takers. The saddest fate we can imagine is to die alone.

Whatever your nut button is, it's going to have something to do with a way in which you don't value yourself. For men, this seems to manifest itself in feelings such as "You don't appreciate me" or "You don't respect me." For women, it's often more along the lines of "You don't appreciate me" and also "You don't love me." But it's the same thing. Once you accept that you have at least one nut button, you can look at your behaviour with your spouse to see how your particular brand of self-not-loving-craziness shows itself.

Let's consider, for example, an all-too common scenario of everyday life. Your mate leaves a towel on the floor of the bathroom.

A fully enlightened person (aka: my partner, Liz) who has no nut button sees this and reacts thusly (spoken while not picking up the towel): "Honey, you've left a towel on the bathroom floor." And the whole thing is over.

Let's pause and make note of something here—the crucial absence of the word "again." The fully enlightened person does not say, "You've left the towel on the bathroom floor *again*." The words "again," "never" and "always" have likely caused more relationship breakups than even, "Honey, everyone gains weight at your age" or "You said it was healthy to acknowledge our attraction to other people."

Those with no cancerous emotional tumours do not use the word "again." For these people, the past is over and forgotten, the future a continual vision of hope.

Next we have a person who recognizes their nut button but has not entirely laid it to rest just yet. This person sees the towel on the bathroom floor and reacts like this:

PERSON WITH SOME GRIP ON THEIR ISSUES (picking up the towel): "Sweetie, you've left a towel on the bathroom floor again and I know, rationally, that you don't mean by this that you have no regard for my life and think of me as a mere servant in our house and relationship, and that it's just my own poor sense of self-worth acting out because of my being a middle child and also my parents always wishing I'd become a lawyer or an accountant, but still, it makes me totally ballistic, so please stop doing it until I finish another round of therapy. OK?"

Finally, we have the person who has no clue that they have a nut button. Being entirely unaware, they will see the world in whatever way most effectively reinforces the issue they don't know they have:

ME (either picking up or leaving towel): "I cannot believe you did this to me again. You never, never think of me and always, always leave your towel on the floor. I am so leaving you for someone who showers at the gym."

✿

There is no doubt in my mind whatsoever, on any level, in any dusty corner or tiny alcove of my being that my ex-husband, Michael, who I will always count as family, was sent into my life to teach me to recognize my nut button. It took eighteen years of marriage, bout after bout of butting heads and egos, hours of therapy (me) and mediation (both of us), 473 self-help books and 693,248 hours of talking on the phone with my sister to arrive at the point where I realize that what was wrong with Michael was simply that he was perfect for me. Perfect for bringing my core emotional issues front and centre in my life. And perfect for exposing to the clear light of day the places where I most needed, not to learn to love him, but to learn to love myself.

Let me offer an example. Michael, for all his many fine traits, has a tendency to...well, let us say, he sometimes allows the size of his commitments to exceed the number of hours in a day during which he could possibly fulfill them. Like many of us, he doesn't always accurately estimate how long the things he has to do are going to take.

Because of this, now and then Michael will call me to say something along the lines of, "I'm really sorry. I had no idea the annual firm budget and critical planning meeting would run longer than fifteen minutes. Can you pick Becky up after her dance class for me?"

This is straightforward enough. Unless, of course, your nut button is "people do not take my life seriously." To me, Michael may as well have said, "I have no regard for your life whatsoever. I certainly don't think you have anything to do that's half as important as this meeting or anything else on my agenda. Really, I believe you sit around all day wearing fluffy slippers, watching TV, eating bonbons and calling it 'writing.' You're so flighty."

This is not what Michael said. Michael would never say these things. Particularly not the part about bonbons. When I examine his actual words, I have to admit that he acknowledges his responsibility and that I'd be doing him a favour. When I think rationally about our history together, I recall that he's been supportive and respectful of my work at every turn. But in the past, I never stopped to examine or think rationally. I'd simply blow up at Michael, screaming like a raving banshee, leaving the poor man wondering what on earth had just happened. I did this because, no matter what Michael said, I heard it through the filter of "other people do not take my life seriously."

Having expended much time, money, anxiety and tears in order to inch my way toward some modicum of realization of my own issues, I am now able, at least some of the time, to hear Michael's request like this:

MICHAEL: "I'm sorry, this meeting is running much longer than I expected. Is there any chance you can pick Becky up from her dance class?" I pause. I remind myself that my life and time are valuable and that, by asking this favour, Michael is in no way suggesting otherwise. I remind myself that I can continue to consider this sort of request as a deliberate personal affront. But, miracle of miracles, I could choose instead to see this as pleasing proof that Michael feels we're good enough friends that he can ask for help when he needs it. I remind myself that there may well come a day when I too underestimate the demands of my schedule and would welcome cheerful, non-judgmental assistance in return. I remind myself that if that day comes, it won't mean I don't respect Michael's time and commitments any more than his request means that he doesn't respect mine. I remind myself that he's still on the other end of the phone and likely wondering why I'm not saying anything. And most of the time I manage to say, "No problem. I'm happy to do it." When I do, my heart sings a little.

I'm not suggesting that the people we're in relationship with are excused from treating us with consideration. But since I've come to recognize my nut button, I have a better shot at determining when an act is thoughtless and when I'm simply interpreting it that way.

Before I identified my issues, it wouldn't have mattered what Michael said or did. I could have been married to Gandhi or the Dalai Lama or Barack Obama or some other guy we imagine is entirely caring and sensitive and I still would have interpreted his words and actions through that filter of my own insecurity. And likely I would have screamed like a banshee. Bottom line, I would have caused myself pain. And then shared it with those around me.

It takes time to recognize our issues. Even then, it's not easy to keep them from running our lives. And, there is only one way to completely heal this psychic sore and rid yourself of a nut button forever. It simply requires many years of practising continual self-acceptance, self-love and remembering to never, ever take anything personally. I haven't managed this yet.

So, is there any point in even trying? That depends. Each of us must decide for ourselves whether the discomfort we'll experience during the slow, difficult process of trying to make different choices is greater than the pain and destruction that will be caused to our relationships and our own hearts if we don't.

It reminds me of a story.

You're walking down a street and suddenly you fall into a pothole. Next day, you walk down the same street and, once again, you fall into exactly the same pothole. The next day, you walk down the same street and think, "Hmmm...I recall that something unfortunate happened here." You fall into the pothole. Next day, you walk down the street, you recall that something unfortunate happened, you see the pothole and, you fall in. Then, you walk down the street, you remember something unfortunate, you see the pothole, you slow down, you fall in. You get the picture. The story continues until one day, finally and at long last, you walk down the street, remember the pothole and even to step around it. Some weeks later, you decide to walk down another street.

Someone commented to me recently that Michael and I had a "failed marriage." I found myself responding, "Yes, but we have a very successful relationship." I can now see that Michael, simply by being Michael, plays an invaluable role in helping me spot and avoid my most debilitating emotional issue. Of course, there are still moments when I find myself tumbling into the same old pothole once more. But then, they don't hang out those "work in progress" signs for nothing.

Siblings, spouses and even ex-spouses are not the only family members that the universe employs to force us to confront our issues. It also uses our children. Just as our brothers, sisters and parents are specially chosen to help us learn, so are our offspring. And, in the Coliseum of the psyche, love for our children is the biggest lion going.

Twenty-one years ago I became a parent. Like most new mothers, I had read all the books, bought all the safety gear, asked all the questions of the birth coach. And, like most new mothers, I was totally unprepared for what parenting would be like. The books can't tell you what you really need to know. For instance, none of them prepared me for how much I would love my child.

Suddenly, the daycare in my office building where I'd planned to drop the baby off at 8 a.m., pick it up at 6 p.m., before getting a babysitter in the evening so I could run errands and keep up with my book club, was out of the question. The moment my child was born, as Michael described it himself, "every cell in my body changed."

I could hardly bring myself to leave my child, even with my own mother (who, I had evidence to prove, was reasonably competent at caring for children) in order to run the hundred yards to the drugstore. A nanny placement worker, finding me a trifle demanding, accused me of wanting a "Mary Poppins." I said that was ridiculous. Mary Poppins was nowhere near good enough for my child. Eventually, I realized I was being far too overprotective. There's a term for parents like this. "Normal."

Over the years I continued to want what I thought was best for my eldest child, as well as the one who came after. There were picnics in the park and tutoring, soccer leagues and birthday parties. Saturday mornings, I stood waist-deep in our community pool, kept at the exact right temperature to provide optimal comfort for penguins, trying to coax one or other of my children off the deck, assuring them that the water wasn't cold, it was "refreshing," as my lips turned blue and I lost feeling in my toes.

I sat through school band recitals that sounded like bull elephants in heat and gushed afterward that a professional orchestra could not have been more wonderful.

And I believed it. I wiped tears and rejoiced over the smallest of triumphs. I helped glue two hundred thousand toothpicks into the shape of a Basque fishing boat and did not once openly curse the teacher who decided that gluing and identifying European ship design were necessary lifeskills. And I tucked my children in each night knowing how lucky I was among parents to know the ones in my care were warm, fed and safe. In other words, I did what any parent does.

Mostly, I simply wanted for my children the same thing all parents want. I wanted the river of their lives to run smoothly. I hoped they would never be troubled by the trials and disappointments that I myself accept as a natural part of my own life.

This brings us to the summer my first child turned seventeen. In describing the series of events in which my oldest child, who Michael and I knew as our son, became our daughter, there are a few things I need to explain. If you haven't parented a transgendered child, what I relate here may be confusing. All I can say is, it's sometimes just as confusing to those of us who have parented a transgendered child.

For those unsure of exactly what "transgendered"

means, the way I explain it is this. My eldest child is a girl. But, for the first seventeen years of her life, we didn't realize she was a girl. The reason is, she was born anatomically male.

At this point, many of you may be saying, very reasonably, "But, isn't that the definition of a boy? Doesn't body determine sex?" Four years ago I would have said, "Yes, of course it does. What a silly question." Now, I'd answer, "Not so much as you'd think."

"The child has a penis, ergo the child is a boy," seems to be one of those irrefutable truths of the universe. Just like "family keeps you on solid ground" or "love doesn't hurt" or "God is good." But like "love never hurts" or "well, God is good, isn't he?" this is absolutely and irrefutably correct right up to the point that you actually apply it to real life. At that point, things become a little more complex.

It seems possible that our identity as female or male is located far deeper than the mere fact of our body parts. Penises and breasts are one way of categorizing gender, but they are not what essential maleness or femaleness is all about.

In the movie *Erin Brockovich*, starring Julia Roberts, there is a moving scene in which Roberts visits a woman who has contracted several types of cancer as a result of contaminants in her town's well water. The woman has had both breasts removed plus a hysterectomy. She smiles tearfully up at Roberts, asking if, without breasts and a uterus, she's still a woman. To which the reply is, "Absolutely." She is a woman, not because she's got the requisite female body parts, but because she's got the requisite female soul.

Writer, teacher and transwoman (a woman born biologically male), Julia Serano, suggests we shouldn't limit ourselves to physical superficialities when determining gender. She contends that it's our spirits that determine if we're male or female. And, that our inner Selves will insist on this no matter which set of genitalia we come equipped with.

To prove how compelling our inner identification of our own gender truly is, Serano asks her lecture students this hypothetical question. "If someone offered you a million dollars if you'd spend your next ten years living, dressing and behaving entirely as a person of the opposite sex, would you do it?" No student has ever said they would. This result, she says, speaks to the reality that we innately know ourselves to be male or female, and, if that identity is repressed, it leaves us emotionally frustrated, twisted and desperate. No amount of money could be worth that.

At the age of seventeen, my eldest child decided not to live a life of frustration or desperation if she could help it. No amount of fear or loss of approval was enough to keep her from being who she is. Jade came out as a transwoman. To me, this seemed extraordinarily courageous. Jade claims it was basic survival.

As I describe what happened in our family, I will use only Jade's current name. She finds it distressing to be referred to by her former name, even when we're talking about the period before she came out. In fact, she doesn't like us to mention her childhood at all. As Jade puts it, "Do you want to remember a time of your life when you were lonely, frightened and depressed?"

At first, it hurt not to be able to talk with Jade about things we'd shared in the past. But I've come to believe that it's not my place to insist that she try to feel differently. When we're unhappy with a situation, we often think the solution is for someone else to change. Sometimes, the answer is to look at what we can change in ourselves.

A professor at the school where I am in training to be a Christian minister has made it his mission to study the best means of achieving respect in interpersonal relationships. He insists that the key is, in fact, to ditch the old Golden Rule, "Do unto others as you would have done unto you." Instead, he introduced his Platinum Rule, "Do unto others not as you would have done unto you, but as *they* would have done unto them." The idea being that it's not sufficient to simply treat someone the way we want to be treated ourselves. Our professor said he realized this after a conversation with our school janitor. The janitor told him that, once a day, he sweeps the common room in our school building. But he noticed that, during high holidays, the Muslim students attending our college use this room as a place to say their ritual prayers. This meant kneeling on small carpets on the floor several times throughout the day.

The janitor was concerned that, since he cleaned the room in the early morning, by noon the floor was already dirty and dusty. He asked one of the Muslim students for a list of their holiday dates. Then, he made a point of sweeping the room several times, just before each prayer period. The students prayed on a clean floor.

For the janitor, it was a small but thoughtful gesture. For the students, it was gratifying evidence that their needs were valued and respected.

"Do unto others as *they* would have done unto *them*." As our professor explained it, I could see that this has to be our goal. And that likely I wasn't up to it. The Platinum Rule is a lot of work. Even the Golden Rule requires us to be as polite and pleasant as we expect others to be to us, something I can barely manage at certain points in my menstrual cycle or when I have a major essay due. When you up the ante to include having the patience, humility and sheer physical time required to figure out what someone else considers respectful treatment, it seemed almost guaranteed that I was going to fall short.

When it came to understanding the needs of my transgendered child however, it was clear to me that the Golden Rule wasn't going to wash. Assuming that Jade's needs were anything like my own made no sense at all. Particularly as, in those early days, my need was for Jade to not take this step at all. Whereas her need was to be her truest, happiest self.

When Jade came out, both Michael and I had to throw out any notions we had had about what was right for our child and, little by little, allow Jade herself to teach us what she needed. In retrospect, this is a useful way to approach any relationship.

At first, the easiest way for me to understand what Jade was feeling was to imagine that somehow her female soul had been popped into the wrong body. Of course, this would mean that the efficiency of management in heaven is about on par with any earthly government bureau. But frankly, by this point, I'd lost some of my ability to be alarmed.

Jade and I now joke that the reason she was ten days overdue at birth was because she was trying to reason with celestial bureaucrats saying, "No, no, I can't go yet! You've made a big mistake here!"

The first thing Jade told me was not that she was a

transwoman. In the beginning, she said she wanted to wear women's clothing.

This was fine. I could cope with this. Michael and I had decided when we became parents that our mantra for our kids' teenage years would be, "It's not drugs, it's not drugs, it's not drugs." Any disturbing behaviour our teens might exhibit, as long as it stopped short of ingesting illegal and mind-altering substances, our plan was just to hunker down and wait it out.

So, when the child I believed was my son announced she wanted to wear women's clothing, I figured that out of the list of what any seventeen year old was likely to say, which might include: a) I'm pregnant, b) I'm driving to Mexico with a guy named Snake, or c) I'm pregnant *and* I'm driving to Mexico with a guy named Snake, I was getting off pretty easy. Jade and I went to Sears, picked out a few items and my child happily wore them around the house.

My younger child, Becky, very reasonably wanted to know why her older brother was wearing a dress. This is exactly the kind of question parenting books never prepare you for. They lead you to believe that "Where do babies come from?" and "Why is Daddy kissing that other woman?" are the trickiest issues you'll ever have to deal with. Parents forced to field "Why is my brother wearing a pink cocktail frock?" should be legally entitled to a rebate on all those books.

At any rate, I had known that my role as a parent was to give my child clear, comprehensible answers to big life questions that I don't have a clue about myself. I said, "I don't know." Later, I managed to say, "It's not drugs."

A few weeks after asking to wear women's clothing, my first child told me that she was a woman. From now on, she wanted to be called Jade.

This was harder. I asked, couldn't she just be gay? I understood gay. In fact, I embraced gay. Not only because I'm homosexual myself, but because gay sons bring home their gay boyfriends. Gay boyfriends adore the mother and want to hang around with her and bake cookies and discuss what was on *Oprah* that day. Gay would be great. I was totally up for gay.

Jade said she didn't know if she was gay but she was definitely a woman.

My child is 6' 3". Until this point she had participated in what I would have called "typical guy stuff." She played video games and liked sci-fi movies. She only had male friends. She'd never wanted a Barbie doll or a Hello Kitty bedspread or a Spice Girls CD. And, she didn't seem to want any of these things now. I didn't get it.

✿

More than that, I didn't want to get it. What I wanted was that placid river running through my child's life. I wanted my child to fit in.

Humans are hardwired to crave relationship. And to learn early the price that must be paid to get it. While we may think we live in a world of individuals, we're still very much pack animals. Stray too far from the norms of the herd and you'll be abused or ignored, left to the ravaging beasts of marginalization and isolation. This is perhaps the greatest cruelty we inflict on each other.

Just how much our pack animal mentality influences our behaviour and makes us desperate to feel we're keeping up with the crowd is something I learned years ago at university. Like most of the really useful lessons we're taught at school, I didn't learn it in a classroom. It happened as a result of an event that seemed inconsequential at the time.

The first week of my final year at University of Toronto, I signed on to staff one of the student orientation tables as a means of making a little extra cash. My job was simple. Students enrolled in first-year biophysics were to come to my table and receive a handout package of class assignments. Then, I was to sign them up for one of ten available weekly lab times. This was not exactly rocket science. It was biophysics. That's meant to be a joke.

Frankly, by the time I'd spent two hours at this task, dealing with a steady stream of Type A, overachieving, superbrainy science-geeks, each one profoundly intense and destined to win a Nobel Prize in something no one can understand, and with about as much ability to just kick back and enjoy life as a turnip, I needed a laugh.

About half an hour into this process, a fellow classmate from the drama department wandered by. I would describe this student as "destined to win a Nobel only if they start handing them out for Possessor of Least Useful Skills Ever Acquired at a Leading Educational Institution." He dropped a small box by my elbow.

"Corks," he announced.

ME: "Go away. I have no time for foolishness." (I shoved the next handout package at the student before me, who looked suspiciously at the box.)

FELLOW DRAMA STUDENT: "I found them when I was cleaning up the props closet. You could use them for...something requiring a cork."

The BIOPHYSICS STUDENT standing before me clutching his handout package, gestured at the box: "What are those?"

FELLOW DRAMA STUDENT: "Corks." (He paused. Then, like the serpent in Eden suddenly thinking it might be amusing to toy with this chick, Eve, and how much trouble could it cause, really?) "Surely you have your cork."

BIOPHYSICS STUDENT: "I don't have a cork. Do I need a cork? No one told me I needed a cork."

ME: "Uh..."

FELLOW DRAMA STUDENT: "You definitely need a cork."

BIOPHYSICS STUDENT (to me, accusing): "You didn't say I needed a cork."

ME: (Make strangled noises which are possibly not helpful or informative.)

BIOPHYSICS STUDENT: "Can I have one of those corks?"

FELLOW DRAMA STUDENT: (Who, I swear, is going to hell.) "These are reserved corks. You should have called ahead for a cork."

BIOPHYSICS STUDENT (turning that deep purple shade a person becomes right before they go into cardiac arrest): "But...no one...no one...told me about the corks. I need a cork."

ME: "Here. Have a cork. Take the cork. This is your cork. And your lab time is Tuesday, 4:15 to 5. Go away now."

The student rushed off, grasping his package and his cork. My fellow drama student left whistling a happy tune, feeling his work there was done.

For the next two hours I was forced to hand out corks

to frantic, overwrought biophysics students who had heard the conversation about the cork and refused to believe, no matter how hard I insisted and assured them that they didn't need one. They were convinced that, sans cork, they were destined to fail the class, be kicked out of school and die alone in a gutter. Those who signed up before the box appeared rushed back panting and panicked. "We heard we need a cork!"

With about thirty students left in line, I ran out of corks. Something close to outright pandemonium threatened. I stood up on my chair and, God forgive me, yelled at the top of my lungs. "Anyone who didn't get a cork can pick one up at the school bookstore tomorrow morning!"

To this day, a part of me wishes I'd been a fly on the wall at the store the next morning or at the first lecture of Biophysics 101 to see the professor trying to make sense of a room full of future Nobel Prize winners clutching their corks.

✿

There is a point to this story. And it's not "there is no task so boring and so mundane that it cannot be turned into amusing oneself at someone else's expense." Nor is it "imagination and guile will beat out logic and sanity every time." At least not entirely.

The point is that all of us, regardless of how sensible, secure and centred we may be, want to feel we're doing what it takes to keep up with the pack. If we lose ground, we may be left behind altogether. So, whether it's choosing the right car, career opinion or wine to serve for dinner, most of us are prepared to work hard and continuously to stay abreast of the crowd.

Pack-oriented behaviour isn't always a bad thing. It's pack behaviour that gives us social order. And our desire to feel we're fitting in, measuring up to the standards of society, is largely what drives our economy. Our individual choices are almost always about what will make us feel acceptable to the group.

I have a friend who buys exclusively designer outfits, so up-to-the-minute fashionable that the knock-off manufacturers are still scribbling them into notebooks. It doesn't matter to my friend what these clothes look like. It may be the year Dior decides the "new black" is actually tassels and feathers, or Dolce and Gabbana design their entire collection around the theme of "circus tent." My friend is convinced that, so long as a garment comes with the right label, she's buying acceptability.

She's not alone. My younger daughter, Becky, wants Uggs. And not fake Uggs. It's easy to tell the fake ones. All you have to do is to lie down on the sidewalk four inches from a person's foot and try to read their heel.

The problem with pack behaviour is that it's acceptance based on...well, being acceptable. When it comes to being acceptable, we can't always manage it.

For parents, this drive to ensure that our kids keep up with the pack can be crippling. I am certain, for instance, that there is a special place in hell for whichever parent first came up with the idea of birthday party loot bags. I suspect I might know who this was.

When I was ten, I was invited to my friend Nancy Ringwall's birthday party. Nancy's family had recently moved from the city and they were considered just a bit too high-toned for our little rural town. Nancy's mother put fresh pineapple chunks in her jellied salad. None of our mothers would have dreamed of offering something so exotic. Canned mandarin orange slices or marshmallows were considered good enough for us. Using fresh pineapple was simply putting on airs.

On Nancy's birthday, we children sat down to the requisite party lunch of hot dogs and carrot sticks. And there, at each child's place we discovered, wonder of wonders, a pink paper cupcake shell filled with glossy jellybeans. It was a miracle of indulgence. We'd never imagined such extravagance existed.

I recall my mother rolling her eyes in derision when I arrived home carefully toting my first "loot." But at every child's party from thereon in, cups of jellybeans graced the table.

I believe, to this day, that Nancy Ringwall's city-suave parents introduced the loot bag to the world. I'm sure they never dreamed of where it would lead. Nowadays, a loot bag, crammed with puzzles, toys, candy, comic books and costume bling, often costs more than we used to spend on a gift and card combined. Recently, I heard of one family who handed out iPods, pushing the benchmark of birthday party giveaways to impossible new heights that most parents can never hope to achieve. They are the Ringwalls of our time.

The reason parents give in to this kind of pressure is not because we're trying to buy ourselves acceptability. We're trying to buy it for our children. This is why perfectly sane, rational parents outfit their kids in Gucci shoes before they can walk or insist they be enrolled in French Immersion classes while their English vocabulary is still limited to "mghhh."

Needless to say, when my own child, Jade, told me she was not simply another of those teenage boys who want to go around the house wearing women's dresses (as my "survival as a parent" brain had been attempting to assure me was possible) I felt a sudden violent shock of despair. My child would never be accepted by the pack. No one can survive that and not end up twisted. She'd be cast out by the world at large. And then I thought, "But not by me."

A few years before this, I had come out as lesbian. The way I now imagine that time of my life is that I was like a lobster. When a lobster outgrows its shell, it sloughs it off. Then it pushes itself under a rock, pink skinned and raw, to hide away from danger until a new shell can form.

The process is the same for any of us when we reveal our true Self to another human being. Allowing someone else to see something honest and raw and real about ourselves, anything we've squirrelled away in the locked boxes of our soul because it seems shameful and unacceptable, is an act of sloughing off an old shell. When we do this, for a time, we're vulnerable, tender and afraid. We stand shivering and exposed, anxiously waiting for our new identity to form. What keeps us safe in the meantime is finding sanctuaries of kindness and reassurance that we are loved and valued by those we hold most dear. We need that protective assurance. We need it immediately. It's not only what shields us in the moment, but also what allows our new shell to form healthily and able to shelter us from harm.

When I first came out, whenever I was introduced to a new group of people I had an uncontrollable urge to tell them I was gay. I tried not to do this. I told myself very sternly that it was really not something other people needed to know. I was fine with it, so I really didn't need to concern myself with what anyone else might think. Also, it was often quite hard to introduce the subject into casual conversation. Inevitably, it caused someone to have to stop and say, "Well, we were talking about China's policy on global warming, but that's very interesting, Anne."

What I've realized since those days is that this irrepressible urge to state who I am stemmed from needing to know if this was a safe place for me. Was I among friends or enemies? Did I have to be careful not to get hurt? My shell of self-love and acceptance was not yet fully formed. I was still looking around for those rocks of safety, ready to push myself under at any time.

Of course the people it's by far the hardest to share our raw real selves with are those who's love and acceptance matters the most. If they judge or reject us, it may feel as if we've nowhere to turn to find protection.

When I came out to my family and closest friends, I met with expressions of love from almost everyone. Almost.

Some might ask, "Well, under the circumstance, 'almost everyone' sounds pretty darn great. Surely 'almost everyone' is enough?" Well, it is great. But no, it's not enough.

One day I met a friend for coffee, a woman with whom I'd shared a close relationship for over twenty years. As clearly and carefully as I could manage, I told her what I'd discovered about myself. There was a long pause. She looked past me. "I think it's disgusting," she said. "Please, never contact me again." Then she calmly stood up, collected her coat and purse and left. I walked home stunned, certain that the hurt and humiliation I felt ripping through my heart would never cease.

Weeks later, this same woman called saying she was deeply sorry for her response. Tentatively, painfully, we began to mend the tattered weave of our friendship. But what I realized was this. Coming out as gay is still an act of stepping dangerously outside the norms of the pack. Those who risk it need other people to love us, not just eventually, but at that exact moment. Because in that instant, it's almost impossible to love yourself.

In the years since I came out, my friends have entirely come to terms with my being gay. My family has welcomed my partner, Liz, as a member of the clan. They rejoiced and celebrated at our wedding, en masse. But this never entirely erased the scar left on my heart, put there by having once been frightened and soft-shelled and having been advised, by someone I counted on to love me, that I didn't deserve acceptance or protection.

I used to wonder if, because of this, there might always be a small part of my new Self that wouldn't form properly. Perhaps there would always be a crack, a tiny fissure that could let in the danger and pain.

I have a friend John who claims the hurts of his past never bother him. After decades of work on his inner self, John says he now pictures all former traumas, issues and what sets off his nut button as a dank muddy bog. "I used to be mired in that muck," he explains. "I was stuck fast. I couldn't move beyond it. I couldn't see a way out." Now, he imagines that he's laid planks over the swamp. "I stand on the planks. I walk over the sludge. It's still there. I can see it. I can even learn from it. But it doesn't touch me anymore. And, it doesn't hold me down."

I tried using my friend's image, imagining laying a plank across the hurt of not feeling loved and accepted. When I was able to stand above the hurt and look at it, I realized it did have something to teach me. I must, if I possibly could, keep this from happening to anyone else. Perhaps this is the best we can do with our most painful issues. Simply try not to pass them on.

My opportunity to turn this policy into practice finally came a full six years later when I decided to ask Liz to marry me. Two weeks before I proposed, I drove the hour and a half to Liz's parents' place to tell them my plan. Glenda and Dave are kind, generous, open-minded people. But I guessed that just maybe I was not the person they'd pictured as the perfect spouse for their daughter. Not simply because I was female. I was also divorced, twelve years older and the mother of two. And perhaps most disturbing of all, I was not the least bit interested in sports. I thought that these two loving parents deserved the chance to wrestle in private with any disappointment or concern they might have for their child's future. Then they could choose how they wished to respond.

I arrived at my future in-laws' house. I had a game plan going in. One I'd learned from my brother, Bruce.

Bruce has never had occasion to "come out" to anyone about anything, except when, after becoming a U.S. citizen, he admitted to our family that he'd voted Republican. I received a warmer reception when I announced I was gay.

When Bruce and I were teenagers, his strategy for asking a girl for a date went like this. He would telephone the girl, opening the conversation with a clear statement of his dating request. Then, he would immediately shift the conversation onto an unrelated topic. This might be a discussion of school activities or music, anything he thought might be of interest to her. Once the young woman had had a few minutes to relax and reflect, Bruce would return to the question of "date or no date?"

This seemed a reasonable method to employ in talking to Liz's parents. I even dared hope I'd have better success with them than Bruce had had with dating.

Dave, Glenda and I sat down at their kitchen table. I said I was planning to ask Liz to marry me. Then I launched into a critique of the new NHL hockey rules I'd read about in the morning paper. Their shoulders relaxed. We were on familiar ground.

Twenty minutes later, having exhausted my store of hockey insights, I returned to the subject of Liz/me/marriage/what do you think? Having had time to think it over, Glenda and Dave were able to express what they really wanted to say which was pretty much, "You look after our girl, or you'll have us to answer to, missy." When I left, they hugged me.

A friend once asked why I'd taken the time to talk to Liz's

parents. After all, Liz was in her thirties and didn't need their permission or even their blessing. I said it was because I once had to tell someone I cared deeply for something it was hard for that person to hear. I had learned that sometimes the people we cherish need space and time in order to collect their thoughts and to sort through their own issues before they can say they still love us. For some people, this takes moments. For others, it might be years. But my need to be instantly reassured isn't greater than my loved one's need to be given that time, space and patience to consider what my announcement meant to them. At the moment you tell someone something real about yourself, it isn't just you that is vulnerable. You both are.

I thought Liz's kind, warm-hearted parents deserved the opportunity to think over their reaction to their daughter announcing she was planning to marry me. Perhaps they needed time to mourn the dreams they'd had for her, so they could open their arms to embrace the ones she had for herself.

What I do know is that two weeks later, when I popped the question and Liz called her parents to say we were engaged, they were happy and excited for her. Liz will always treasure their enthusiastic response.

When Jade came out to me, I didn't have time and space to consider my reaction. I couldn't pause to mourn my dreams or sort out my feelings. I couldn't stop to ponder how I'd feel after I'd wrestled with my fear. What I could do was to call on my own painful, precious experience of knowing exactly what my daughter's soft, scary, pre-shell state felt like. And how desperately my child needed to be told that she was loved. Not for being any particular way. Not for meeting any of my expectations or doing what it took to fit in. But unconditionally. Just as she is. Simply because she exists.

So, Jade told me she was a transwoman. I opened my mouth to speak. I told my child that I loved her entirely. That she was wonderful. That she was more than acceptable, she was perfect exactly the way God made her. And that I was ready and willing to support her in whatever she wanted her life to be.

I don't remember much about the next few minutes. I think we held each other. We must have cried a little. Jade may have said she was relieved. I'm sure we were both fearful. But mostly, we were excited and joyful.

I can't recall anything after Jade spoke those words

and I heard myself, without hesitation, respond. Until suddenly, I felt a surge of thankfulness welling up from deep inside. It was gratitude for the hard, painful lesson that had equipped me to help my child. And with it came the shell-shattering sensation of becoming whole again.

Years ago, I read a line in a book that made no sense whatsoever. Now I understood. "Sometimes love can travel back in time and heal a broken heart." There are moments in life, perhaps few, but some nonetheless, when the suffering of our past rises up and helps us to make something new and good of the present. For me, this was such a moment.

The next stage of Jade's coming out occurred a few weeks later. The guidance counsellor at the high school where Jade was in grade twelve called to say that my child had announced she was planning to start attending class wearing women's clothing. At that point, my brain exploded.

I don't know what I'd expected when Jade announced she was a transwoman. Perhaps I should have anticipated this. But frankly, that's a little like saying that if someone mentions that the stars are beautiful, you should expect them to start building a spaceship to head for the moon. How do you prepare yourself for something you can't possibly be prepared for?

I'd learned to negotiate the world from the margins as

a lesbian. I'd handled my kid's coming-out speech. Heck, I could have offered classes on handling a kid's coming-out speech. What more was I expected to deal with? I was beginning to feel as if my life was a giant cosmic poker game and God was announcing, "OK, I'll see you being lesbian and...I'll raise you a transgendered child."

I had no idea how to help a child who is 6' 3", has always been known as male, was currently student council president of her school, the largest high school in the city, and who's decided she'll now go to class dressed...well, in a dress. There would be no missing her. I was terrified for Jade's safety, not only bodily but emotionally as well. Life is hard, even for those who do manage to conform to the pack.

The only thing I knew for sure was, someone had to tell her father.

Michael and I live on the same street. This is one of the benefits of overcoming your disappointment and anger when you divorce. Sometimes you're able to live close enough to each other that forgotten textbooks, and children not being near their friends, in their own neighbourhood, are among the issues you don't have to deal with.

Now and then someone asks, don't I mind having my ex-husband living just three blocks away? I can only assume these are people who have never came to the end of an exhausting evening only to realize that the beloved stuffed dog/cat/whale/frog/something-that-used-to-be-a-dog-but-has-been-hugged-into-a-grey-pulpy-sponge without which your child cannot possibly be coaxed into going to sleep, has been left at the other parent's house. At that point, I promise you, letting go of anger and disappointment seems a small price to pay for not having to drive across the city wearing your pajamas.

Jade hadn't told Michael she was transgendered because she hadn't needed to. She lived with me and saw Michael for movies, school events and for dinner twice a week. I hadn't told Michael, because I believed it was important to keep Jade's confidence. Eventually, when she was comfortable with herself, I knew she would be ready to tell her father. Now, apparently, Jade was comfortable enough with herself to go to school in a skirt, but she still hadn't told Michael.

✿

Jade's guidance counsellor and school principal were expecting Jade's parents to come to a meeting the next morning to discuss our child's plan to wear women's clothing at school. Not telling Michael was no longer an option. Jade said she couldn't do it. I would have to.

All Canadians know a story about our former prime

minister, Pierre Elliott Trudeau, and a particular long dark night of his political soul. In 1974, the city of Montreal seemed in the grip of terrorist activity by the FLQ. Trudeau was forced to consider instating the *War Measures Act*. This meant calling in the army to patrol the city and giving them extraordinary authority to invade the privacy of ordinary citizens. In a country where we pride ourselves on civil rights, this was a drastic, unprecedented action. For Trudeau, a champion of rights and freedom and a native of French Canada himself, taking such action must have been almost unimaginable.

Legend has it that on that fateful night, Trudeau left the Prime Minister's residence on Sussex Drive and walked out through a silent wintry evening. Step by step he made his way to the home of the Governor General, the official empowered to proclaim the *War Measures Act* at the Prime Minister's request.

Trudeau trudged slowly, amid softly falling snow, consulting his conscience—asking himself, "Is this the only possible course?" and knowing that what he was about to do would change the country forever. He must have agonized, "What should I do? What should I do?" Or, I suppose, *"Que dois-je faire? Que dois-je faire?"*

The night I received the call from Jade's school, I felt a kinship with Trudeau. I walked the few blocks from my house to Michael's. Light snowflakes were falling, lit up under the glow of the streetlights, like tiny stars.

I trudged up the hill, wondering, "What should I do? What can I possibly say?" I've called Michael the nicest guy you could hope to be divorced from. He's a good man, gracious to me and supportive of our children. Despite our divorce, there was always order and comfort in our family. And, he'd been so proud of our son. Nothing I had to say that evening was going to alter the history of my country. But it was going to change Michael's life forever.

I arrived at the house. Michael and I went into the living room. We sat down. I explained as carefully and clearly as I could what Jade had told me about herself and what she now wanted. I finished talking. Michael sat in silence.

Since the day Jade came out, I have learned many things. I have experienced sensations more moving and intense than anything I ever imagined was possible. Not only extreme sorrow and fear, but also extraordinary, almost profound thankfulness and overwhelming joy. None of these emotions came close to what I felt next.

My child's straight father, who had never had the difficult, invaluable lesson of coming out to anyone about anything, who had been proud of his son for seventeen years, consulted his heart for one very brief moment and then asked, "What do I need to do to show her I love her?"

Twenty minutes later, Michael was back at my house, enveloping his eldest child in a big bear hug of support. I watched in wonder, knowing I would never see anything more awe-inspiring. I was in the presence of true and unconditional love.

Doctor, author and wisewoman Elizabeth Kübler-Ross said that unconditional love does not mean loving when we understand, but loving when we don't. Often, at our Transceptance group, the new parents who seek us out are bewildered by what their child has told them. I recall one of our more experienced members rising from her seat during a meeting and moving around the table to take the hands of a newcomer. Looking into the father's tear-stained face she said, "Don't worry about understanding. Understanding will come later. Or, maybe it won't. Just concentrate on loving. That's the part that matters." The Platinum Rule.

I don't think, in those first hours, Michael understood what Jade was experiencing any more than I did, and I had known for weeks. He just concentrated on love.

The next morning, Michael, Jade and I went to Jade's school. We were ushered into a room where we found the school principal, Jade's guidance counsellor, Dale Calendar, and also a social worker, a vice-principal and a woman I swear to this day was introduced to me as the district officer for "adolescent abnormality," though Michael assures me it was "youth life coach."

Michael and I agreed the night before that we had two concerns to discuss. "How is the school going to help Jade with this transition?" and "What can we do to keep her safe?" We were not prepared to debate coaxing Jade to wait six months before taking this step, until she started university. She'd be away from home then, in a new environment with no familiar support systems. Besides, Jade had made it clear that she'd already waited as long as she could. Nor were we going to entertain the suggestion that she go into counselling for gender confusion. She'd been seeing a therapist for years. And, as Michael put it, "She's not confused. She's a girl."

The school principal began the meeting with these words. "Thank you for coming this morning, Mr. and Ms. Hines. We want to discuss two concerns with you. First, how we're going to help make this transition as comfortable as possible for Jade. And secondly, how we're going to keep her safe." Michael and I looked at each other. It felt like a miracle.

Dale Calendar had a plan for introducing Jade to the school in her new persona. He'd prepared a written statement for all teachers, explaining what "transgendered" meant and suggesting ways they could relay this to their students. Dale would be with Jade for the whole of the first day for moral support. He would make himself available after each class to talk to students and teachers who had questions or concerns. Dale explained, "This isn't just about Jade. When one person changes, everyone around them has to change." There are many kinds of families.

Finally, Dale said he'd consulted with local police about how to keep Jade safe outside of school. She would carry a cell-phone and alternate her route home each afternoon.

Michael asked Dale where he'd found the ideas that went into making this plan. Dale said he'd done online research, consulted youth guidance manuals and read through a stack of teen sexuality books. There was no mention anywhere of how to help a transgendered student integrate into their school system. "So I made it up," he admitted. "But I'm thinking of writing it down." He did. Dale Calendar's manual is now in use by educators and guidance counsellors helping transyouth come out in schools all over the world.

All this time, my head had not stopped exploding. I would wake up each morning with fireworks going off behind my eyes. I went to bed at night unable to sleep before soft yellow light began to filter through the bedroom shutters. I lay silently in bed, wondering how Liz could be snoozing so peacefully when Armageddon was being played out on the pillow next to her.

To be fair, the only way Liz could have known what I was feeling would have been for me to tell her. I couldn't. I couldn't tell anyone. OK, sure, as Jade went off to school wearing her favourite peach skirt, most people might have suspected that I was a little on edge. But I didn't tell anyone that every moment of every single day, I was terrified for my child's safety and happiness.

I was also ashamed. Not ashamed of Jade. She seemed a miracle of courage to me. I was ashamed of myself. I was ashamed of my own feelings. I wanted that peaceful river in my child's life. I was sure that fitting in and being acceptable was the way for her to find contentment. I was forced to remind myself sternly that sometimes what we convince ourselves our child needs is, in actual fact, simply what we ourselves want.

Michael and I went to Becky's school, just down the road from Jade's high school, to explain the situation. We asked her principal and teachers to watch out for her and make sure she was OK. The conversation felt surreal. Each time I had to tell someone, "Our child is a transwoman," a voice screamed in my head that this couldn't be happening, certainly not without the world coming to an end.

Weeks passed. Rockets continued to burst. The Fear Brigade was still holding regular rifle practice in my forehead.

A parent of one of Jade's classmates, meeting me on the street, snapped, "Why don't you get your child a good therapist?"

I barked back, "She has a good therapist. How do you think she got to this point?"

Some parents (but no students) lobbied the principal to have Jade removed from being school council president. They argued she was no longer the person their children had elected to represent them. The principal refused, noting that the school president doesn't have to be approved by the parents. And, that the qualities and abilities that got Jade elected had nothing to do with her gender. "So," he said, "Since gender is the only thing our school president has changed about herself, I don't see that we've got a problem here." Jade continued to run meetings and speak on behalf of her school at public events.

All this time, I was sure the universe was trying to teach me something through my child, but whatever it was, I really didn't feel like hearing it. It would have been impossible anyway, with my mind exploding like a minefield.

One evening, four or five months after Jade had come out to me, Liz and I took an evening stroll through our neighbourhood. On one front lawn, someone had placed a large plywood stork, one of those signs that can be rented to announce the arrival of a new baby. "Oh look," Liz said, "they had a boy."

I replied, "Well, they think that now. It ain't over till it's over." We laughed.

In that twinkling of cheer, I felt a sharp inner tug. Surprise. And then, the sudden shock of astonishment that occurs, often seemingly too soon, after a devastating loss, perhaps at the end of a marriage or the death of someone you love. This is the instant you realize, to your great amazement, that the world did not end. You've continued to live. You can almost breathe again. You've remembered how to laugh. In that split second, we transition. Into hope.

Atheists point to the presence of suffering in the world to prove that God must not exist. I look to the constant, assured return of hope as proof that God absolutely does.

The morning after our walk, I got up and realized I'd slept almost the whole night. The artillery fire in my head had diminished. I was astounded to realize that whatever colossal, life-altering event occurs, the sun still rises the next morning. The world continues to turn. It just looks a little different than it did before.

Jade's school newspaper ran a smart, respectful article on the change in their student body leader, ending with, "Best of all, after seventy-five years, our school finally has its first female student council president."

In place of the brain explosions, I now felt overwhelmed by an even more persistent sensation, continual astonishment at the kindness I found everywhere. Neighbours stopped by. They said, "Tell Jade we're so happy for her" or "She's always welcome at our house." People I'd never met came up to me on the street, saying, "Tell Jade we're right behind her." Others, who'd read Jade's story in our city's newspaper, sent e-mail messages of support and encouragement.

I began to wonder if, having been so entirely fixated on the trials of the situation, there might be other blessings I hadn't noticed. I was beginning to realize that the thing about difficult life events is, you can see the bad things easily. The bad things are right out there. They're in your face. You can't miss them. The blessings may need to be looked for. But they're there as well. Sometimes just a little hidden, like sweet summer strawberries beneath prickly green leaves.

Becky arrived home one day saying a group of boys had yelled across the schoolyard, "Hey, you're the freak's sister!" Some friends, and a few classmates she barely knew, had immediately closed ranks around her to provide protection and comfort. Becky added that one or two girls she'd been pals with now avoided her altogether. She said, "Mom, you almost need to have things like this happen, don't you? It shows you who it's worth being friends with."

I joined Transceptance. The fact that such a group existed startled me into awareness of how many children are born in the wrong body. Now, once a month I meet with a room full of parents who, like me, are sorrowing, terrified, but also hoping like all get out. We share stories, tears, laughter and hugs, bound tightly together by how much we care for our kids. We hold hands, encouraging each other to let go of our plans for our children's lives, so that we can begin that all-important task of hearing what they dream for themselves. To me, this still sometimes feels as if I'm staring into that psychic pothole once more. I wonder how many times I'll have to walk down that same street before I finally, entirely, stop thinking that I know what my children, or anyone else needs, and learn to wait to hear them name it for themselves.

At Transceptance, we remind each other that we have been given what, as parents, may be the greatest blessing of all. We have the chance to show our children we love them. Not because they're acceptable to the world. And not because we understand them. But unconditionally. Simply because they exist. And that sometimes, family can be a soft place to land, a rock solid support, as well as being what challenges and transforms us.

✿

Three years after Jade came out, Michael and I sat side-by-side in a ballroom packed tightly with celebrants decked out in crisp tuxes and glittering evening gowns. Pride Toronto's annual gala awards dinner, a sumptuous affair. No one throws a stylish event like a group of gay men.

We watched proudly as Jade made her way onto the stage to accept the Youth Leadership Award. Later, she commented, "Mom, they gave me this award for just being who I am." I told her that sometimes that's what it takes to be a leader.

Standing before several hundred people, including our provincial premier, Jade began her acceptance speech with, "I wish someone had told me ten years ago that it was possible to transgender. And that you could even get a prize for it." This time, the only explosions were laughter. By the end of her short talk, the audience was on its feet, applauding. And Michael and I weren't the only ones wiping away tears.

Watching my daughter delightedly make her way back to us through handshakes of congratulations, bright, confident, her face flushed with pride, I wondered, "Who would not choose this?"

Three years before, Michael and I had had a choice. Not about whether or not Jade would come out. She had to do that. And not about whether or not we'd change as a result. We had to do that. We're family after all. Biologically tethered together. And certainly not a choice about whether or not we loved our child. That was born into us.

The choice we had to make was whether or not our love for our daughter came without conditions. If we'd chosen differently, insisted that she do what it took to remain acceptable...well, I don't know what would have occurred. We chose to try to love.

Have we loved without fear? No, not always. Without concern? Almost never. But certainly, I think, always with determination and faith. And without conditions. And now here was our daughter, joyous and strong, celebrating who she truly was, and inspiring other people to risk being whoever they are as well.

Liz, who has no issues, says that life is about loving. I, who have many issues, say it's about learning to love.

✿

This reminds me of a story.

Two elderly monks and a young novice leave their ashram one day and walk all the way around to the far side of a large lake to meditate. Just as they're sitting down, one of the older monks says, "Oh dear, I've forgotten my prayer mat. I must go and get it." So, the older monk trips off across the lake, stepping right over the surface of the water. He arrives at the ashram, goes in, gets his mat and comes walking back across the lake to join the others. The young novice is agape at this. Then the second elderly monk says, "Oh dear, I have forgotten my prayer beads. I will go and get them." He too goes trotting off over the lake, the waters not even rippling under his footsteps. The second older monk comes back the way he went and the three sit down to meditate. The younger monk can hardly believe his eyes. He thinks, "Surely I am as enlightened as these two fathers." So, he says to the two older monks, "I have forgotten my...my incense. I will go and get it." The young novice steps out onto the water and immediately sinks in up to his armpits. Then the first older monk turns to the second and says, "Do you think we should show him where the stones are?"

In the waters of life that so rarely run smoothly for any of us, unconditional love makes up the stones beneath the surface. It's what sustains us and holds us up, along with kindness, hope and the knowledge that blessings exist, even in those times when we have to look hard to find them. This is where we can place our trust when the way seems precarious and uncertain. It's what allows us to continue simply putting one foot in front of the other. Which, I think, is often the best we can ever do.

I don't know what challenges and changes life still has in store for me and for my children. But this I do know. The sun always rises. Life continues, just sometimes a little differently than you expect. Hope returns. And I now know that the purpose of family is not simply to support you, but also to transform you. Which is even better.

So, in the end, I didn't lose a son, I...well, yes, I lost a son. But it's been more than a fair trade. I gained stones beneath my feet.

III
Losing Confidence

Tsunamis of the Soul

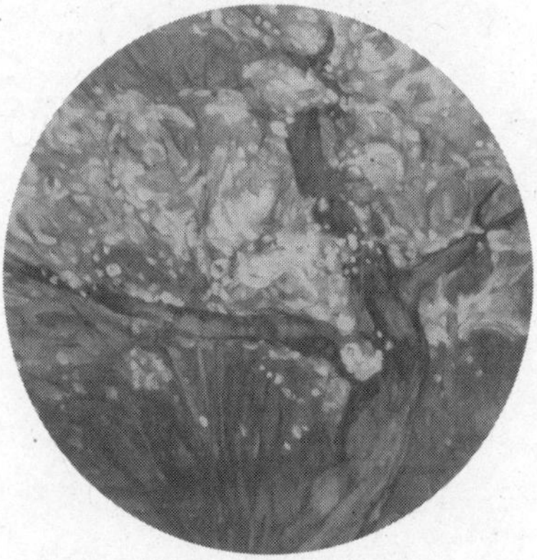

A FEW MONTHS AGO, I made a definite, solemn, unbreakable vow. I decided I was giving up the business of writing forever. Never again would I apply pen to paper or fingertips to keyboard. Never. Not under any circumstances. Even, if my life depended on it. Or the lives of the people I love. Or, the existence of the entire free world. Like say, for instance, if space aliens invaded the earth, and threatened to suck our blood out or blow everything to bits, just like a scene from a bad Tom Cruise sci-fi movie: "Unless the Hines human dashes off an eight-hundred-word piece on WHY WE REVERE SPACE aliens." Not even then. I was signing off on the whole writing thing. For good.

There could only be one circumstance that would compel me to make this kind of statement, of course. I'd been hit by a tsunami of the soul.

Life is like this.

One morning, you're sauntering to work, thinking, "Well, things are not so bad right now. I'm a valued, respected member of my corporate team. I've mastered the fundamentals of personal growth from reading one deeply meaningful self-help book. I've perfected a clear, individual fashion style: "urban-country-classic-but-still-really-out-there-chic...with a little 'flirty'...but not so much I catch cold...or have to wear heels. Or, God help me, a thong. Best of all, I'm finally over that emotional hump with my [insert boyfriend, girlfriend, spouse, mother, therapist, hairstylist here]. Yes, it's all working out at the moment. I believe I will even hum a little." And you do.

This, as we all know, is just asking for trouble.

As the saying goes, "The gods don't like to see mortals too happy." That day, Human Resources invites you to a meeting to discuss what else you might do for a career. A petition lands on your desk, signed by the office vegetarians, demanding you stop circulating inspirational quotes from *Everything I Need To Know About Life I Learned from Poultry Farming*. Someone asks if your new fashion statement means you've joined the Amish. And, the [boyfriend, girlfriend, spouse, mother, therapist, hairdresser] announces that, in fact, they don't find you the most beautiful, intelligent and fascinating person on the face of the earth which, as everyone knows, is their job.

Suddenly, doubt comes crashing in like a tidal wave. In one swoop, it topples your self-esteem and washes complacency and contentment so far out of your life they're floating somewhere near Tahiti by the time you come up for air. You've been hit by a tsunami of the soul.

It takes very little to trigger a tsunami of the soul. A stranger makes an unkind comment. A friend commits a small slight. You get a bad performance review. Or you momentarily forget that advertising wasn't created for the purpose of assuring you you're lovely just as you are, but to insist that you are not perfect at all. Nor, for that matter, is your hair, your weight, your retirement strategy or your cell-phone plan. And the sooner you get out and purchase a ninety-dollar teeth-whitening kit, the better. One thirty-second clip suggesting, "You'll never be an adequate parent if you don't use a bathroom cleaner that could sterilize a nuclear waste dump," and an averagely confident person can be knocked sideways by a wave of uncertainty.

How is it that reasonable, self-assured people can be levelled by these sudden bouts of low self-esteem? The answer is, of course, that no reasonable person has much self-esteem at all. History is littered with tales of those who achieved fame and glory, were acclaimed by all around as being talented, accomplished and adored, yet who succumbed to feeling poorly about themselves. Marilyn Monroe doubted her looks. Beethoven questioned his musical ability. Mother Teresa, who had every right to think of herself as doing pretty well in the "being a worthy person" department, suffered frequent bouts of depression and misgivings. If these luminaries couldn't escape the tsunamis of the soul, is there hope for the rest of us?

Human beings seem fundamentally designed not to feel good about ourselves. Perhaps this is simply nature's way of ensuring our survival. Any Neanderthal who announced, "Sure that sabre-toothed tiger is powerful, but I'm way tougher," was almost certain to have his contribution to the gene pool discontinued fairly promptly. But it's hard to fathom what Mother Nature had in mind when my dazzling teenage daughter obsesses that she isn't smart enough, attractive enough, popular enough, thin enough. I'd love to be able to teach her what a waste of energy this is, but I'm too busy worrying about the same things for myself.

The truth seems to be that no one on earth—however gorgeous, talented, brainy or svelte—has not, at some point or other, been blindsided by a tsunami of the soul. It's a commonality we diverse human beings share. We have all, on occasion, been witness to our sense of self-worth being carried off and whirling down into the dank sewers of despair. When that happens, nothing can save us. Not anger or umbrage, booze or Botox, assurance or shopping.

On the surface, the solution to never experiencing a tsunami of the soul seems obvious. Never have a job, talk to other people, talk to yourself, enter into relationship, go out of the house or own a mirror. I didn't say it was a good solution.

About six months ago, I suffered a significant tsunami of the soul. A giant monolith of self-doubt smashed onto my psyche like an ocean breaker laying waste to a sand castle. I was knocked down. Hard. "Ass over elbows" my friend Gigi would say.

My personal tsunami of the soul had to do with my work as a writer. A novel I wrote received a scathing review in a national newspaper.

When I finally floundered to the surface, I was devastated and humiliated. I made up my mind I was never going to risk having this happen again. So, there was only one sensible course of action. I must stop writing altogether.

This was not the first time I'd come to this decision. Like most writers I know, when I complete a book, I swear I'm going to switch careers rather than put myself through such emotional bloodletting again. I think it was Mark Twain who said, "I hate writing. I love having written."

When I finish a writing project, I always dream of a career at Dairy Queen. Not only does dipping ice cream into chocolate seem like a simpler life and altogether greater service to humankind, I have a sneaking suspicion the pay is probably better.

Writing a book has often been compared to giving birth. Few women having just made it through the sweaty arduous hours of labour declare, "I sure hope I get to do this again—soon." I, for one, was wheeled from the birthing room swearing I was not setting foot outside the hospital until they'd had my husband fixed.

By the end of any writing venture I'm exhausted and muddled. I no longer have any idea what the book is about. I'm not sure I care what the book is about. And, I'm feeling entirely unappreciated by my evil, evil publisher who won't let me have the one little thing I need to make this book really good: four more lifetimes.

Then, incredibly, a new idea springs to mind. Often it happens within just a few days. The pleasure of having something fresh to think about returns. "I'll never write again," morphs miraculously into, "I'm so, so lucky to get to do this and I hope my fabulous, kind, supportive publisher will say 'let's give it a go.'"

The difference between my usual "I'll never write again" vow and the one made a few months ago was, of course, that I'd finished a book months before. It was on store shelves. The pressure was off. I'd got past the point of thinking that a better world lay at Dairy Queen. Reawakened to the joy of having a new project to immerse myself in, I'd remembered that life is sweet and so is the job of writing, and that my publisher is wonderful, kind, supportive and a blessing to my existence. I may have even been thinking, "Well, things are not so bad right now." Perhaps I engaged in a little contented, inner humming.

At exactly that moment, the newspaper ran the savaging review of my book. And, a tsunami of the soul high as a skyscraper swept down. Nothing could save me. Every grain of my contentment and self-esteem was dragged far out to sea.

I tried telling myself that everyone in the world has, at some point, been blindsided by a bad performance review. Mind you, not everyone's bad review was printed in two million newspapers for people to peruse over their Saturday morning coffee.

Dorothy Parker, in a *New York Times* book review, once famously suggested, "This is not a novel to be tossed aside lightly. It should be thrown with great force." Parker's assessment was a rave compared to what was said about my book.

The critic hated my theme, my prose style, my characters, my opinions, the colour of the book jacket, my clothes, my taste in music and my mother. She might not have actually mentioned those last few things but it certainly felt implied.

Worst of all, she didn't find a single line or passage of my book even remotely funny. I think it was Stephen Leacock who observed that you can tell a man he has no beauty, no morals and even no intelligence, but say he's got no sense of humour and you'll really give offence.

I was shocked, ashamed, embarrassed. I asked the

friend who had called to tell me about it: "Wasn't there anything at all about the book she liked?"

"Well, of course," he said, "there's always...hmmm...no, there really isn't."

"But don't worry," he added, "likely no one will read it."

"The review or the book?"

"Maybe both."

Another friend called. She reminded me I was lucky to get reviewed at all. She insisted that most readers only remember the names in stories but forget the details. I said, "Oh yes, like with Charles Manson. Or Hitler."

As I went about my day, I was convinced that everyone was talking about me. The nice gentleman who owns our cornerstore. The bus driver. The seventeen year old who sells me coffee. They were all thinking, "Oh yes. She's the one who wrote a really, really bad novel." My neighbours, who appeared to be absorbed in cutting their lawns or chatting about the weather, were actually murmuring, "Wow, she got the worst review in the history of the world. Ever."

My partner, Liz, insisted, "Honey, no one cares that you got a bad review." I wasn't sure if I found this comforting or more upsetting.

I carried the humiliation of this review around with me for weeks. Finally, I decided it was time to take mature, reasonable action. I made the vow to simply never write anything again.

I telephoned my publisher, Kim, to inform her that I was never writing another book, even if my life depended on it. I also described the space-alien scenario. I hung up the phone feeling, "This is good. This is right." Perhaps now I would get a real job. If not at Dairy Queen, at least somewhere where I would not be the object of disrespect and a complete lack of appreciation. Perhaps, retail sales.

I had already worked part-time in retail. Over the past few Christmas seasons, I'd helped out in the kitchen store where Liz is manager.

For someone who normally works from home, this was a kind of dream job. Eight hours a week, I got to get out of the house, wear clean clothes and talk to other people. Best of all, there were definable goals. "Go get a stand mixer and sell it to this customer," someone would say. I would race down to the stockroom, haul up the stand mixer, take the customer's money and be filled with the extraordinary, previously unprecedented satisfaction of actually having completed an objective. Very different from writing, where the goal "create good stuff" is murky at best.

In addition to all this, my family could now ask, "How was work today?" I work every day, of course. They meant real work.

Writing doesn't look like working. Often, it looks like gazing out the window beside my desk, watching sunlight filter through the emerald green leaves on my cherry tree. Now and then it looks like taking a nice hot bath. Or, it looks like taking a long walk through the park or watching raindrops slipping down the sliding doors on my back deck. Mostly, it looks like sitting in front of a blank computer screen.

Writing is like a relationship. The key isn't so much being able to handle the highs and lows. It's being able to stay with it during the times that nothing much of interest seems to be happening at all.

The largest part of writing is simply bringing yourself to the page. Sitting and waiting. If you go and do the laundry you won't write a word. If you plant yourself in front of the screen or hold the notebook in your lap for an hour, fingers hovering over the keyboard or pen poised above the page, you might, if you're lucky, end up with a sentence. Mind you, the laundry will still be dirty. You know you're a writer when this isn't a tough choice.

There are two things you have to come to grips with as a writer. Well, three if you count not making any money—but for some reason that seems the easiest to accept.

The first thing is that most people will never believe that you do any actual work. Unless, of course, you write a bestseller or are employed part-time in a kitchen store. And, perhaps hardest of all, you will never be as wise as what you write. I have no idea why this is, although a few of my characters have explained it beautifully. I do know that it's true.

Henri Nouwen, for example, was a modern-day Dutch theologian who wrote emphatically, beautifully and incessantly on the topic of what our highest duty on earth might be. Nouwen insisted that we are here to learn to love—love each other, love God (or whatever our concept of the divine might be) and, perhaps top of the list, love ourselves, because it makes other kinds of love possible. What we are not here to do, he stated, is to chase after the transient, unsubstantial approval of the world. This simply distracts us from what constitutes true, abiding, transforming love.

Nouwen wrote these things with great sincerity, intelligence and commitment. He also suffered regular, debilitating bouts of depression because of his frantic desire for the very same attention and approval he assured us we should have no truck with whatsoever.

Now, it could be argued that Nouwen's depression was simply the obvious result of being both Dutch and a theologian. With either one of these, you're almost guaranteed an excess of earnestness. I'm not saying that the Dutch don't have a lighter side. I am saying there may be something in the fact that they've produced many intense, moody artists such as Van Gogh and Vermeer, but no famous stand-up comics. Some countries are known for some things and not others. No one sitting around in front of the TV on a Friday night, for example, ever says, "I'm feeling a little peckish. Let's send out for Belgian." Or, "Gosh, I could really go for a tall frosty French beer right now."

The point is Henri Nouwen was not as wise as his work. No artist is.

Hanging above my desk is a poster of Van Gogh's painting of sunflowers. Each bloom is a glorious, fiery burst of orange and gold. Each stem is buckled and bent. This is the ultimate affirmation of life. In spite of our brokenness, the artist assures us, this is still a beautiful world, forever full of vibrant possibility and passionate hope. Van Gogh painted this. Then he killed himself. He was not as wise as his work.

French Impressionist painter Monet said, "I believe in God when I work." I think he meant that when we engage in an act of creation, sometimes, suddenly, we find ourselves painting or writing or thinking something finer and wiser than we know ourselves to be. It's as if a trace of the divine has managed to slip by our anxious, censoring brain and push its way into the world. When that happens, it renders us awestruck. In that moment, creative activity has entered a strange, mysterious universe. It has become like golf.

Every golfer I know claims there is one thing that keeps them from finishing up each round by putting their clubs on eBay and swearing off the game entirely. It is this: for every hundred horrifying, disastrous shots that end up in a lake, a sand trap, up in a tree, or out in the parking lot lodged in someone's windshield wiper (I saw my ex-husband, Michael, do this once, so I know it's possible), comes a swing when everything works like a dream. The ball flies straight. Effortlessly. As if angels are guiding it. Then it plumps down firmly and exactly on the spot intended.

A dedicated golfer will suffer years of shots that slice, dribble and otherwise find their way into remote and embarrassing places, just to experience that mystical, perfect swing once again.

✿

On a flight to Calgary years ago, I sat beside a young man I recognized as an Olympic long jumper. He looked the poster boy for *Obsessively Committed Athletes Monthly*. Clear-eyed, clean-shaven.

The young man politely declined the airplane meal,

explaining that his fitness regimen dictated he eat only high fibre, high protein nutrients and not greasy indeterminate yellow stuff we'd been assured by the flight attendant was quiche. Instead, he invited me to share his stock of kelp balls. I declined with equal politeness, feeling it would be wrong to take kelp balls away from a youth in training. He detailed for me his "nutrition regimen," that seemed to consist mainly of ingesting things I might normally use to fertilize my lawn. He also had a "toning regimen" designed to fine-tune muscles I don't believe I possess.

I asked, "When do you know that you've made a good long jump? When your feet leave the ground? At the arc of the jump?"

He answered, "Most of the time I know when I take off." He paused. Then, he leaned toward me, flushing slightly and whispered, "But sometimes, there's this thing that happens. I jump. And suddenly it's like everything around me has disappeared. I can't hear anything. Not the crowds screaming. Not my coach yelling at me to tuck tighter. Not even my own heartbeat. It's like I'm being carried through the air without having to do a thing." He sat back. "When I land, I've gone farther than other jumps. But it doesn't matter how far I went. It's the silence. Being lifted outside myself. That's why I keep jumping."

✿

It's the longing to experience that same extraordinary bolt of transcendence that keeps the rest of us golfing, painting, dancing and writing. In writing, that flash of the sublime occurs just about as frequently as a perfect golf swing. A single phrase tumbles out fresh, smart and perfectly formed. Or a line takes shape laboriously, gradually like damp clay plied by patient hands, melded slowly into something that says almost exactly what you know in your heart to be true. And with it comes the all too fleeting impression that we've been lifted out of our own fears and limitations, touched something both deep inside and far beyond ourselves. These are rare, astonishing moments. Humbling. Sacred. Ecstatic. They're what keep me going.

✿

In the days after I received the bad review, I forgot all about that. I was in the grip of a full-blown tsunami of the soul. I forgot there was anything that made the difficult business of creating worthwhile.

I was beaten. I was a fraud. Certainly, I wasn't a writer. A newspaper critic had said so.

Despair drowned both hope and perspective. Liz would say, "I think this weekend we should stain the deck" and I would think, "The world has ended. And, I am a bad writer." Or, my mother would call and ask, "How are the kids?" and I would think, "I am a bad writer. Likely a bad parent too."

A friend who also writes once sent me a stickie note to post above my computer. It reads, "Don't judge." Now and then I would pass through my workroom, not planning to sit at my desk ever again. I'd see that note and mumble, "I'm not judging. It's a fact. I'm a very, very bad writer." Another time I noticed a memo I'd tacked to my bulletin board. It says, "You only live in this world once." I thought, "Good thing, too." I lugged my feelings of hurt, disgrace and degradation around like extra body weight.

One day, weeks later, I ran into an old friend on the street. She immediately began relating how upset she was over something the man in the condominium unit next to her had said. The two had met in the elevator. My friend's neighbour mentioned how annoyed he becomes when people leave their discarded sofas, appliances and other large recycling items behind the building for the weekly municipal pickup truck to collect, instead of making private arrangements for them to be taken directly to the dump. To his mind, this is sheer laziness and makes the parking area look cluttered.

My friend was horrified. He was accusing her. She was sure of it. He didn't say he was. She certainly wasn't going to ask if he was. She was sure of it anyway.

She talked on and on, insisting to me that she has never, ever left a sofa in the parking lot. Not for a minute. Not half a minute. She didn't even own a sofa. She did have two small loveseats. And, if she ever planned to get rid of them she would certainly never dream of doing anything other than renting a van and taking them immediately to a landfill. Or, she'd drive them to Goodwill. She certainly wouldn't arrange a pickup. She'd never want the Goodwill truck coming and cluttering up the parking lot. I suggested this didn't make a lot of sense. She replied, "I know? Can you believe what he said?"

My friend raged on. It was outrageous of her neighbour to accuse her of blatant, premeditated antisocial recycling-related behaviour. Likely, he'd told everyone on the floor that she abandons large pieces of furniture in the driveway. Maybe he'd told everyone in the whole complex. She would probably be hauled up before the next condo board meeting. She'd have to move out. She could never hold her head up in that building again. It was unfair. It was cruel.

I decided it was time to lure my friend away from this topic onto another, more important issue that needed to be discussed. Such as how unfair and cruel it was that I had got this really awful book review.

ME: "Don't take this personally. He's probably upset about something else altogether. It's got nothing to do with you. Now what this critic said was..."

MY FRIEND: "Don't pay any attention to that. It's just one opinion. But can you believe what that man said? He actually thinks that..."

ME: "He's a jerk. You're a perfect neighbour. It reminds me of this newspaper review I was telling you about..."

FRIEND: "You got slammed in a newspaper. Try getting it from the person who lives next door. What he said was..."

I gave up. Some people just can't see beyond their own issues.

I stood listening to my friend rattle on. This was ridiculous. Anyone who knew her could attest to her being neither lazy nor antisocial. How could this smart, sane woman be pummelled into emotional mush by one casual comment?

Suddenly, I was struck by a thought. Maybe my smart, sane friend wasn't upset because her neighbour said something she considered untrue. Perhaps she was feeling outraged, shamed and devastated for another reason altogether. She thought it was true. She believed it. Not the part about leaving items outside in the parking lot. She knew that was false. What she believed was that she *was* capable of doing this. She believed, in spite of all evidence to the contrary, herself to be inconsiderate, slovenly and, most important, not worthy of being a member of the group.

A new idea began to dawn on me. Perhaps what sets off a tsunami of the soul isn't the bad reviews we get from book critics or apartment neighbours. Just maybe, the real cause of a tsunami of the soul is the bad reviews we give ourselves.

✿

I was reminded of another friend, Rob, who had recently received his annual performance review at work. We met for coffee and, fighting back fierce annoyance, he tossed me a copy of the critique to read. Rob's boss had said, "Rob is a responsible, creative, intelligent contributor and a valued and respected member of our team."

Rob glared across the table. "Can you believe it? After all I've done for that company?"

I re-read the review. To my mind, his boss's glowing comments stopped just barely short of announcing, "Rob is adored and admired by all. The man is a hero. We don't know where we'd be without him. We're just lucky, lucky, lucky," followed by a long list of reasons the company would go down the tubes entirely if it wasn't for Rob being on the face of the earth and, specifically, with their oh-so-fortunate organization.

I suggested to my friend that possibly, just maybe, he'd lost his mind. He pointed to the page. Far down, near the bottom, underneath a three-paragraph-long treatise on why Rob deserved to get the next and biggest promotion the organization had to offer, were the words, "Rob's work would be improved by learning to use his time somewhat more efficiently."

"I have a good mind to quit," he said bitterly. "If that's the kind of lousy treatment I can expect."

Walking home later, having secured Rob's promise that he'd call me before he hit "send" on the pithily worded letter of resignation he'd spent the morning composing, I wondered about my two friends' reactions. It seemed to me that the criticism that had knocked them both sideways had one thing in common. It was entirely a product of their own mind. I wondered if, in fact, perhaps any comment, even those that truly are cutting and unkind, will simply slip off us like dry rice off satin so long as we don't think it's true. When it sticks, when it bores into our souls like a tic beneath the skin, it means one thing only. We believe it.

What my friends and I believed, what we actually heard the boss, neighbour, book reviewer say was this: "You're not valuable. You're not worthy people. Other people are far, far more worthy than you are." They didn't say it, of course. But that's what we heard.

So, the job review wasn't the problem. The recycling-bin comment was beside the point. The appalling book review that seemed glued to my spirit like cosmic flypaper was beside the point as well. What matters isn't what was said. What matters was what each of us believed. And what will turn anyone, no matter how gifted, gorgeous or grounded they may be, into blithering, emotional pulp. It's the sudden overwhelming conviction that we are not valued or valuable. Not worthy or worthwhile. Not loveable or loved. This is what causes a tsunami of the soul. It's also what's laid bare when the tides of criticism sweep through. This is the basic eternal unadorned pain of being human.

And it all goes to prove one thing. Maimonides was right.

Maimonides was a Jewish philosopher in Egypt in the twelfth century. Mostly, he wrote about religious law and doctrines and how very, very important it is for us all to go about slaughtering our goats in the correct manner. But Maimonides also had many good things to say about how people may learn to live gently and well with each other and with themselves. He was a great sage. Picture Oprah wearing a robe and turban, sitting atop a camel, and you've got Maimonides.

Maimonides devised a metaphor for the kinds of emotional and physical pain that exist in the world. He pictured pain as a single pyramid, divided crossways into three sections.

Maimonides suggested that the peak of the pyramid, the tip—that is, the smallest bit—represents one kind of pain in the world. This is pain that is a result of simply being human and having a body. The trials of sickness and old age, the mortality of those we love or our anguish over our own limited lifespan go here.

The middle band, the second largest part, shows the suffering we cause each other. This would include, though is in no way limited to, neglect, cruelty, unkindness, hatred, intolerance, being judgmental, or any other action that detracts from someone else's safety and dignity.

The bottom band of the pyramid is by far the largest. This is the suffering we cause ourselves. This may be through worry, self-doubt, envy, covetousness (this is an ancient word meaning "wanting a chalet or an iPhone because everyone else has one...they really do") resentment, anger, putting yourself down...anything by which you attack your own sense of contentment and value.

The message of the two lower bands of the pyramid taken together is: "Almost all hurt that exists is caused by human beings. We can do something about it." In other words, if the world isn't Eden, it's because we don't choose it. It also illustrates that the greatest part of suffering any of us experience is what's inflicted on ourselves by ourselves.

There's an old saying, "Neither God nor the Devil can cause us half as much pain as we cause ourselves with our own thoughts and behaviour." Listening to my friends express their pain, in almost the same words I used to describe my own, I realized this is entirely true.

The root of my self-doubt wasn't the newspaper review or the newspaper reviewer. The source of my suffering was my bad opinion of myself. Discovering this was entirely freeing. And alarming. At the same time.

Viktor Frankl, another on the list of "totally amazing and brilliant Jewish thinkers" survived internment in a Nazi concentration camp. He insisted that, "Everything can be taken from a man but one thing, the last of human freedoms—to choose one's attitude in any given set of circumstances, to choose one's way."

What I realized was, I had a choice. I could continue to tell myself I was untalented and unworthy. If I did this, I would be morose, miserable and not write. This wouldn't be much fun. Or, I could choose to start trying to give myself better reviews. Unfortunately, this isn't quite as easy as it sounds.

A Buddhist master said that all human beings need and desire the same thing. We just go about finding it in different ways. What we all want, of course, is to feel valued. It's through cultivating a deep, abiding sense of our own inner worth and value that we build the dikes of our self-esteem strong enough to keep us safe when a tsunami of the soul sweeps through. But this is hard to do. Feeling valued comes from feeling loved and appreciated. Largely, the world seems designed not to allow us to feel this way. We can't always count on receiving the appreciation and support we need from other people. And it's an even more dicey proposition to expect to get them from ourselves.

I've often wondered about the Biblical commandment "Thou shalt love thy neighbour as thyself." Usually this is interpreted as meaning, "Treat other people as well as you treat yourself." Frankly, if I treated my neighbour the way I treat myself, nobody would be speaking to me by the end of the day.

I would never go next door and suggest to my neighbour, Cheryl, that every annoying trait her child displays is a result of inferior parenting. But if my daughter Becky is ten minutes late for curfew or leaves her homework until the morning it's due, I certainly tell myself it's my fault. When my children do something amazing and wonderful or display an admirable trait, I assume they were born into the world with it. When they fall a little short of those qualities, I'm convinced it's because I'm a bad mother.

It's also true that I wouldn't stop a colleague at work to mention what a lazy slug she is because she can't seem to lose those last five pounds. The glamorous French actress Catherine Deneuve once insisted, "After a certain age, a woman can have a great face or a great behind, but not both." I contend that a little softness around the hips makes a woman look sensuous and sexy. But let me catch sight of those pounds on my own body and I'm condemning myself for being not lush but lumpy.

To my mind, the famous Biblical commandment should not read, "Love your neighbour as yourself," but rather "Love your neighbour way, way better than you love yourself because frankly, sweetie, you're not always very nice to yourself." And while I can see a rationale for our built-in feelings of caution (Saber-toothed tigers/survival) it's difficult to understand what nature had in mind in instilling a tendency not to value ourselves.

I have known people who have bought themselves a lot of things. That isn't valuing yourself any more than buying children everything they want is loving them. In many cases, it deprives them of the chance to aspire, achieve and feel joy. I've known people who made themselves the centre of every event. And those who were constantly kvetching about how hard done by they were. Neither of those is valuing yourself. I've known, and more than occasionally have been, the kind of person who always had to be right or to have the last word. That's not love for myself, or the person I'm speaking with. In fact, I'm firmly convinced that in any love relationship, the better part of caring is not how often we manage to say the right thing but how often we manage to simply shut up and say nothing.

Some express their lack of self-value by putting distance between their true selves and others in hope that no one will find out how unworthy they are. Others try to get to the root of the self-not-lovingness by discussing it with a therapist. My father used to insist that "anyone who'd see a psychiatrist should have their head examined," but in a time when we call in a specialist to change a dimmer switch, it may not be unreasonable to seek professional help to change ourselves.

Consulting a therapist is not the same as simply talking over your fears and failings with a friend. Friends give you advice. They tell you exactly what you should do. A therapist studies for many, many years and learns many things so they can sit back and let you figure everything out for yourself. Besides, I've always said I don't pay a therapist ninety dollars an hour just to listen to my problems. I pay them ninety dollars an hour so I don't have to listen to theirs in return.

By the time I got the bad newspaper review, I'd already been to several therapists. I was able to identify all the unhelpful and unattractive ways my personal lack of self-love played itself out in my life. I had also determined whom I might possibly be able to blame it on. This last part took some real in-depth psychological sleuthing. Traditionally, a woman is allowed to blame her husband or ex-husband for everything, including, but in no way limited to, wrinkles, world wars and water retention. My ex-husband was nothing but kind, helpful and supportive. Just my luck. Similarly, I couldn't blame my mother. She's a wonderful, caring person.

One therapist and I settled on my blaming my lack of self-assurance on my eighth grade phys-ed teacher. I don't truthfully remember experiencing any problem with my phys-ed teacher. I do remember that our school's standard gym uniform for girls was a puffy, cotton, one-piece, royal blue "romper." Today, any teacher who demanded that self-conscious teenage girls appear in public in that kind of get-up would be hauled before a human rights commission faster than you could say "suspended without pay." The gym romper must have left a mark.

It wasn't until years later that I hit on the real reason for my sense of self-unhappiness. I'm human. I might have been more elated at discovering this answer if I hadn't immediately reflected on how many dollars and hours it took me to get it.

After all this analysis, the one thing I still didn't know

about my shortage of self-esteem was how to get over it. I decided to get off the couch and into the library. I am a great believer that there is no problem so thorny or so complex it can't be solved by a well-trained librarian who knows which section to direct you to.

I was delighted to find that, when it comes to locating the path leading to self-love, a few human beings have actually discovered the way. And they left directions.

Writer Helen Keller was born deaf and blind. Given this, one might assume she had every right to feel bad about herself and her situation. Yet, Helen Keller became renowned for her joyous, upbeat approach to life and authored some of the most inspiring optimistic words in existence. Among these is, "I do not fear storms. I'm learning to paddle my boat."

There it was. If I wanted to rise above the tsunamis of the soul, crest those waves of self-doubt and fear, I needed a lifeboat. And, in a world that all too often doesn't provide me with the feeling of being valued that I need, and where safety, love and appreciation seem in short supply, that lifeboat would have to be learning how to provide these things for myself. The keyword here is "learn." It's a lifelong lesson.

Put another way, learning to value ourself means being our own parent. Not just any parent, but someone who isn't afraid for us and just wants us to do our best. It's being the parent who encourages us to follow what makes our heart sing and not worry so much what the rest of the world thinks. In other words, it's being for ourself the parent we never had and can't quite manage to be for our own kids.

Or one could picture it as being our own grandparent—maybe the perfect grandmother who sits you down in her newly scrubbed kitchen with the mottled, slightly slanted linoleum floor and clean white curtains luffing on a spring breeze. She places a glass of cold milk in front of you. Maybe it's in a Spider-Man glass, or Cinderella. She passes you a warm cookie.

Then she says something like, "Honey, you're the most wonderful, beautiful, amazing being on earth." And you believe it. Maybe she follows this up with a little gentle advice. You can hear it, because you know it's love. "Do your best, and then forget about it." Or "Eat properly, but have a cookie now and then." Perhaps "Get some sunshine. So, it wrinkles your face a little. It smoothes out your spirit." And "Don't worry too much about what the world says about you. They don't know you like I do."

Nelson Mandela is a world-famous advocate for freedom and peace and a writer who was also the brunt of unfavourable criticism. In Mandela's case, the critics threw him in jail, terrorized his family and threatened him with execution.

Mandela survived his ordeal with his positive spirit intact. He went on to say and write such uplifting thoughts as, "Our deepest fear is not that we are inadequate. Our deepest fear is that we are powerful beyond measure. It is our Light, not our Darkness that most frightens us. We ask ourselves, who am I to be brilliant, gorgeous, talented, fabulous? Actually, who are you *not* to be? You are a child of God. Your playing small does not serve the world."

Generally, I am not extremely comfortable with telling myself I am gorgeous, talented, fabulous. But clearly there's a problem associated with needing to have others say it for me.

Also, I am not entirely comfortable with the God word. This might be considered a tad odd for someone studying to become an ordained minister. My future career is as a professional in the God business. It's the word I find tricky, the actual name "God," that I have concerns about. It's hard to escape the image of a white man with a white beard wielding a whole list of criteria titled Thou Shalt Not that lays out exactly what it takes to receive love and the assurance that we're valued. Criteria I am never going to be able to live up to.

The general concept of god I have no trouble with at

all. That there is a wiser, higher, more loving power than myself seems, to me, beyond question. What exactly this power might be, it is generally agreed, is something we humans, with our limited minds and language, can never hope to fully know and define. Then, of course, we try to define it anyway. This is where trouble starts.

The reason we need a word for this "thing" is simply, of course, because we need a common language in order to talk about it. If one person called the power "Phyllis" and another person called it "small foreign automobile," or "steak with all the fixings," talking about the god thing would be even more confusing than it is already. So, many of us agree to call it "God."

The God word comes with a lot of baggage. Even more than "used car salesman" or "politician" or "mother." Say those words and they conjure up distinct images of what they represent. In the same way, it's hard to hear "God" without also assuming many layers of meaning. For many of us, these meanings include religious cruelty, oppression and intolerance.

Wiccan writer Starhawk calls the divine "Goddess." She describes it by saying that when she feels strong, the goddess is something inside her. When she feels weak, the goddess is something outside of her. I think she means that in those rare and precious times when we feel strong, grounded and centred, it's as if we've tapped into an inner wellspring of energy that suddenly shines out braver and more powerful than our frightened, fragile selves. The divine is inside us. But in the times that we feel weak, lost or bowled over by self-doubt brought on by the tsunamis of the soul, we need to feel there's a source of strength outside of us as well. We need something or someone we may call on to give us the hope and courage we can't, at that moment, find within. At those times, the divine is that grandmother we can't always be for ourselves, holding us close, assuring us that we're remarkable and capable and so, so valuable simply because we exist. I once heard a minister suggest, "If God had a refrigerator, your photo would be on it. If God had a wallet, your photo would be in it." The perfect grandmother indeed.

✿

The truth is, I need to write—just as other people feel compelled to paint, sing or dance. Writing is my connection with myself. It's how I go about figuring out the world outside and inside. It's where I find my God. Just as playwright George Bernard Shaw found connection to the divine through gardening. He said, "You are closest to God in a garden. You can dig for him there." Some people find God through long walks or doing yoga. It's one of the ironies of our world that this ancient tradition, designed to promote an appreciation for non-attachment to worldly things, now comes with exercise outfits starting at two hundred dollars. You can't buy access to the divine.

✿

The Celtic mystics believed that we each hold within us a "deep knowing." They insisted that human beings are born into the world with an innate sense of what we need in order to live in contentment and in communion ourselves and with the god thing. A famous Celtic Christian monk named Pelagius preached that there was no need for priests or church buildings, religious doctrines or rules. What we need, he suggested, are simply "soul friends."

A soul friend isn't a trained authority figure. It's simply another searching, struggling human—someone who walks beside you on your life journey, providing companionship and support, helping you stay courageous in the face of life's ups and downs, and encouraging you to hear and trust your own inner voice of wisdom.

Pelagius wandered around the Celtic world insisting that God doesn't live in buildings or rules, but in our own hearts. He insisted that the divine can be accessed by anyone at anytime.

Eventually the Church hierarchy in Rome, men who made a business out of buildings and rules, conjectured that if the masses became convinced that all anyone truly needs is a soul friend, there wouldn't be a bright future for their profession. So, the Church authorities announced that Pelagius was a heretic. They branded him "an enemy of God." Pelagius was forbidden to preach and share his ideas.

The result of this event was that the world got more church buildings and whole rafts of religious doctrines and rules, as well as the priests and church hierarchy needed to enforce them. But the Church was often a little short on encouragement to develop a personal relationship with God. It had nothing at all to say about the possible benefits of hearing and trusting the wisdom we carry within us.

A psychiatrist friend once told me that, after several decades in the profession, she's convinced that every person who comes into her office already knows the answer to the problem they're wrestling with. Some are having trouble accessing the part of themselves where the answer lies. For others, the difficulty is accepting what they know. My friend says that her job is to be a kind of soul friend. She helps people hear and honour their own inner voice. She supports them as they engage with the wisdom they hold within.

It's possible to be your own soul friend. It just

requires a quiet activity that allows your mind to gently wander and reflect. For some, like Bernard Shaw, this is possible when gardening. Others take those long drives. If you do this, country roads are best. It may be entirely possible to talk to your higher Self when barrelling down a crowded highway, but it's almost impossible to concentrate and listen.

Waiting for the bus is a good time to talk and to hear. So is standing in line at the grocery store. People worry that our busy, modern world leaves no time for quiet reflection, but frankly, if all the time I had to commune with my Higher Self was in store checkout lines, there are days I'd be logging more prayer hours than a cloistered nun.

Most often, I access my inner answers through writing in my journal. I once heard myself telling someone, "I don't know what I think until I write it." In a way, my journal is my soul friend. Many people have suggested, "Isn't a journal just you talking to yourself?" I believe, in it's best moments, it's me talking to God. What makes me think this? I am not as wise as the answers I find there.

So, when I'd finally exhausted myself with my own emotional haranguing and become bored of the pain of self-pity, I limply decided I was ready to hear something beyond the really nasty reviews I was giving myself. I took a few deep breaths and sat down with my notebook. I said a prayer to whomever or whatever might be listening. I asked that I be taught how to regain my balance and find that all-important love for myself. Perhaps, I might even discover a way to keep from being knocked "ass over elbows" by every criticism that comes my way. I hoped to learn how to paddle my boat—a boat that would carry me above the tsunamis of the soul.

I sat down with my journal. I asked the only question I could think of. Perhaps it's the only question we ever need to ask.

"What do I need to know now?"

The response that flashed into my mind floored me. It was, "Why do you write?"

✿

It's human nature to always want a little more than what we have, to feel that complete happiness and fulfillment are always just slightly beyond our reach.

When we obtain a goal, most of us immediately set the bar a little higher. This is not always a bad thing. It's this desire to go further and to improve on what we have that has given us such highly useful things as penicillin and indoor plumbing. Without our innate drive to advance, humankind would still be out hunting for leeches or a nice cushiony spot in the woods.

On the other hand, the continual yen for more can

be unhelpful. Recently, I visited a friend who was recovering from having a surgical eyelift. I asked if she was pleased with the results. Her response, "Absolutely. But you know, my neck looks terrible..." I understood entirely. I once decided to buy new towels for the bathroom and ended up redecorating the entire house.

In this same way, most people who write, I think, hope to get published. Those fortunate enough to be published hope to be reviewed. Next they hope for great reviews. Then to get published again and, this time, to have a bestseller. Then to win a Governor General's Award. Then a Man Booker Prize. Whatever we do or achieve, most of us continue to place the carrot of fulfillment just slightly beyond our own noses.

When confronted with the question, "Why do you write?" I had no clue what the answer might be. I suspected, though, that it had something to do with this idea of fulfillment. But it felt bigger than winning a Booker. What was bigger than a Booker? Selling your movie rights to Tom Hanks and his wife perhaps.

While I share the dreams of many writers, eventually I began to wonder if the real question wasn't "Why do you write?" It was "Why do you do anything?" I didn't know the answer to that either.

Concentration camp survivor Viktor Frankl championed the notion that the fundamental quest of every human being is to answer one cosmic question, "Why do we do anything?"

During his internment, Frankl observed that, among those who weren't forcibly killed, a few people did manage to hang onto life in spite of the extreme physical and emotional horror and deprivation. But, Frankl noted, those who survived were not necessarily the ones who were young and brawny and had arrived at the camps at the peak of health. Many of these captives died early on. Others who were physically weaker managed to fend off disease and despair for much longer.

Frankl determined that what made the difference between living and dying seemed to come down to one thing. The people most able to withstand extraordinary hardship were those who had a sense of purpose.

Some inmates had a profession they were determined to return to, work they were convinced no one else could do. For others, there was someone left behind who loved and depended on them, who needed them to stay alive and to someday come home. In every case, it was a feeling of being of particular value that seemed to sustain these men and make them determined to keep going.

Frankl became convinced that a sense of purpose isn't simply an important component to life. A sense of purpose, he said, is the most essential factor in what keeps us alive.

On some level, we know this. Most of us can imagine taking a job that offers less money but high personal satisfaction. There's even a general consensus that occupations such as social work, art or teaching, should come with a smaller paycheque, because a strong element of self-fulfillment is part of the compensation package. People who think this, by the way, are usually not social workers, artists or teachers.

We all want to be paid well, but we also need to feel that what we do with our time and talent matters. My friend Rick is an architect. Rick loves his work but is driven to distraction when clients ask for meaningless design changes. It doesn't matter that he bills by the hour. If the task is foolish and unnecessary, Rick can hardly bring himself to put drafting pencil to paper.

Some people work at jobs they don't love because doing so serves a loftier, more meaningful purpose. For some of us, this higher purpose is paying rent and eating. My friend Marni, a musician at heart, works full-time for a financial institution because it serves a greater purpose in her life. Marni owns a wool-eating cat.

"Gimlet" lives to hunt down Marni's knitting basket from the back of a closet, the top of an armoire or wherever Marni has decided "the cat can't possibly find it there," in order to swallow whatever stringy substance she can get her little cat jaws around. She has even extracted spools of thread from Marni's sewing machine and attempted to swallow them whole.

On the occasions that Gimlet proves herself smarter than her owner, the stringy substance must be surgically removed from her stomach by the vet. Even with Marni's pet insurance company coughing up a thousand dollars a pop (unlike Gimlet, who never coughs up anything), the bill to make Gimlet string-free can still be as high as two thousand dollars.

Marni loves Gimlet. She loves every furry cat cell in her little cat body. But, of course, people whose joy in life includes loving a wool-eating cat can almost never work at places that aren't financial institutions. That's OK. Deep inside her musician soul, Marni knows why she's there.

One of the worst things you can do to a human being is take away their sense of purpose. Studies have shown that someone who is fired from a job and replaced by another worker will have significantly better morale than someone who's let go because their position is deemed unnecessary.

As I write this, my younger daughter, Becky, is preparing to leave for university. The big day is four weeks off. I've already started weeping. Partly this is because I'll miss her, of course. But also, I admit, it's because parenting my two girls has consumed a large portion of my time and attention for more than twenty years. If I'm no longer going to be doing the mother thing full-time, I'm going to have to rethink what my purpose in life might be.

✿

Doctor Elisabeth Kübler-Ross became internationally renowned as the physician who "brought death out of the closet." To my mind, her main contribution to the world was as an advocate for living with purpose.

As a young hospital intern, Kübler-Ross was shocked at how dying people were treated by the medical profession of her time. Often patients were not informed that their diseases were terminal, and even more often, they were ignored and received significantly less time and care than patients who were expected to become well again.

Dr. Kübler-Ross wondered if the source of this abysmal treatment was embarrassment. To the world of science, death is not simply part of the natural cycle of life, but it is an adversary of medical technique and knowledge. Every person who dies is a failure for modern medical science.

Dr. Kübler-Ross believed that the process of dying is in fact a necessary part of learning to live. She insisted on bringing terminally ill patients into her classroom to share their feelings and experience with student doctors. These patients taught a new generation of doctors how to provide respectful, compassionate palliative care.

Kübler-Ross found that her patients were eager to share their thoughts and feelings. Through helping the students learn, the patients felt that their experiences had both value and meaning. Some, she felt, enjoyed an increase in energy and even extension of life because of it. Most importantly, all of the patients she interviewed or invited into her classroom seemed to die in a more profound state of peace.

After many decades of work with the dying, Kübler-Ross became convinced that each of us has a purpose to serve during our time on earth. She believed that we are all here for one reason: To learn how to love. Others. Ourselves. Our God, if we have one.

Until that purpose has been completed, Kübler-Ross insisted, at least to the best of our ability, we must continue to live. She used her mother as an example.

Kübler-Ross's mother was an extremely energetic person. She was always cooking and cleaning, caring for her family, the first to step in and nurse a friend or relative through an illness or help a neighbour in need. Late in life, this active, vital woman became seriously ill and was confined to her bed. Soon her condition deteriorated further. She existed for years in a non-responsive vegetable state.

Kübler-Ross's mother had begged that if such a thing happened steps be taken to end her life. Her daughter refused. She believed that, in her dependent state, her mother was providing her friends and medical team with the opportunity to care for her just as she had cared for others. And that her mother was being forced to learn the other, sometimes hardest part of love—to let others give to her. Kübler-Ross was certain that her mother would die at the point when her learning had been fulfilled.

Ironically, Kübler-Ross's own last years also involved severe infirmity. She too often wished for death.

Near the end of her life, a journalist with a camera crew in tow came to visit the aged doctor, hoping to capture for posterity a few last words of wisdom. The journalist was outraged when she arrived, only to be told that Kübler-Ross did not intend to keep the interview appointment she'd made. At first, Kübler-Ross wouldn't even let the reporter into her house.

The woman complained bitterly about this experience in her next book. She'd gobbled up Kübler-Ross's compassionate, insightful work on the meaning of life and death. She'd come on this trip, almost a pilgrimage, it felt like to her, expecting to be welcomed into the presence of a gentle sage. To be illuminated and inspired. Instead the journalist was confronted with a self-centred, cantankerous old bat who didn't give a hoot about the reporter's dreams, disappointment or how much it cost to bring a camera crew from Canada to New Mexico. The woman left, seething and disillusioned.

But at the core of the books the journalist loved is the idea that all of us must learn and serve our own purpose, even when it means not serving those around us. Perhaps after a lifetime devoted to the observance of other people's living and dying and serving other people's needs and desires, Kübler-Ross's purpose in those last difficult years of her life was to get to know and serve her own. Focusing on her own needs, fulfilling her own purpose was more important and pressing than meeting the expectations of a journalist.

For many women in particular, the idea of putting our wishes and needs first is a radical idea. I was taught to understand that the definition of love is "how much I manage to give to others, and not to myself." For most of my life, I believed I was the sum total of two things—how much I accomplished in a day and how largely the things I did contributed to the comfort and convenience of those around me.

My faith tradition, Christianity, has done a good deal to support this notion though we are by no means the only religion to do so. Christianity's take on the meaning of personal value, at least as women are taught to understand it, has often been that only when she has baked all the brownies, arranged all the flowers, comforted every tear, worked on every committee, met every need of every person she comes in contact with, generally made the world a better, nicer place to be, and done it all without complaining, gaining ten pounds or resorting to Prozac, only then has a woman given enough...or almost.

To my mind, Kübler-Ross's greatest teaching couldn't have been caught on any cameraman's tape. It wasn't what she'd learned about meeting the desires and ambitions of others. But rather, that she insisted on honouring and fulfilling her own.

Why do we do anything? What is our purpose? This wasn't the first time in my life I'd been presented with a question of cosmic importance for which I had to search for an answer. But for some reason, the process of finding one hadn't become any faster. I sat with my journal. I stared at the blank page. It remained blank. I took long drives. I walked. I waited. It is so hard to wait. I listened. I read. I listened some more.

One Sunday morning, I was sitting in church listening to the minister recount a story about Jesus's disciples, and wondering, as usual, why the worst things always seem to happen to the people with the most faith—Jesus, Moses, Luke, Mary, the list goes on.

Suddenly, I was struck by divine lightning.

All of life comes down to one thing. Every search for meaning and purpose, the quest to find and know love, the secret to feeling safe and valued and to finding enduring protection from those tsunamis of the soul that threaten to knock us sideways—everything Viktor Frankl was trying to tell us and what Kübler-Ross learned from other people's dying and her own—the answer to "Why do you write?" and "Why do we do anything?" It all comes down to one thing. Actually, it comes down to one story. One Bible story. Not about Jesus or the disciples. About a man named Job.

This is the story.

ACT ONE: We are introduced to Job.

Job lives in the land of Uz. I have no idea where Uz was, except that it sounds like the capital ought to have been the Emerald City. I do know that Uz seems to have been a town of considerable size because it was large enough to employ a small army of city officials, our man Job being one of them. Apparently there were many things to be decided in places such as Uz. I have no idea what these might be—maybe where people were allowed to park their camels.

Right from the get-go, the story of Job is rather odd. Job, we are told upfront, is a gentile. This is unusual because the Bible almost never features non-Jews in leading roles. This is particularly true in the Old Testament. Being a gentile in the OT is like being an extra in a *Star Trek* landing party. The OT is very concerned with the trials of Jewish people and generally relegates gentiles to minor parts where bad things happen to them. Being a gentile in the OT means you're pretty well guaranteed that at some point the Red Sea is going to come crashing onto your chariot or you're going to get wiped out by the relatives of Esther who happens to have a particularly good "in" with the king, or you'll be whapped in the forehead by a rock launched by a small boy with a slingshot, and die. Bottom line, if you're a gentile in the Bible, things are not going to go well.

The next thing we hear is that Job was "perfect and upright...and eschewed evil." So far, he sounds like many of us, right? I for one certainly eschew evil. If evil presented itself to me right now, my response would be, "I eschew you!" Mostly, I just like saying, "eschew."

The fact that Job eschews evil sounds good, but describing him as "perfect" is clearly a red flag. The writer is setting us up for something. No one is perfect. Although I have to say that in spite of being convinced that I'm of no value whatsoever, I also have moments of thinking I'm far better than other people. Particularly when I'm driving. If someone cuts me off in traffic it's because they're horrible, insensitive trolls. If I do it to someone else, it's because I am a lovely, thoughtful person who just happens to have her mind on some higher purpose at the moment.

The point is Job can't be perfect. So, why is the writer of the story saying this? Our interest is piqued. It's like a Biblical thriller.

Job has seven sons and three daughters who, and this is where you can tell this is a made-up story and not historical fact, all get along beautifully. Apparently, Job's children were in and out of each other's tents all day long, sharing each other's good fortune, feasting with each other's families and not one of them griped that it was someone else's turn to do the cleaning up or complained about each other's kids.

We assume Job had a wife as well, though the Bible doesn't mention her at this point.

Next we learn that Job owned a whole whack of livestock. This, next to sons and daughters, was the best thing a man could have in those times. And, we're told that Job was very conscientious about his religious duties. He made all the right burnt offerings at just the right times. He made sure his children did too. Job was staying on the right side of God.

So, there is Job, just trucking along, living pretty much like the rest of us. Well, maybe a little better than the rest of us. Job's got amazing kids, financial security and he's considered a big shot in town. He holds down a position of authority. People clamber for his advice. He gives money to the poor. Bottom line; Job's got it all going on. Perhaps, he even hums a little. And we know where that gets you.

Disaster strikes. Everything in Job's life goes sadly awry. Well, it appears to go sadly awry. There is certainly a sadly-going-awry sort of look to what happens next. But just before it begins to go awry, the storywriter gives us:

ACT TWO: Heaven.

It's another beautiful day in eternity. God is sitting around visiting with the angels. They're talking about, I don't know, maybe how ugly those dinosaurs were and what was God thinking when he made them anyway and how humans are just as strange but at least they do interesting things with their fingers.

Satan arrives. According to the Bible, he just shows up. Walks in unannounced. But God doesn't say, "Oh my Self, Satan!" God is quite blasé about the whole thing. Leading one to believe that they must visit this way all the time.

God says, "So Satan, where've you been? What you been doing? Who've you seen?" And Satan, who, thanks to the movies, we know looks like Elizabeth Hurley, just as we know that God looks like George Burns or, according to Michelangelo, an old man with a long beard, or maybe rather like Santa Claus who, thanks to Coca-Cola, we know, is pink-cheeked and white-haired...anyway...

Satan answers God saying, "Well, I've been down on earth just walking around, you know. Doing this and that. Convincing humans they need things like weed-free lawns and religious doctrine. Why do you ask?"

GOD: "I was wondering if you noticed my friend Job while you were down there."

SATAN: "Job? City counsellor, seven sons and three daughters, whack of livestock, revered by all, gives alms to the poor? Or, Job the pomegranate salesman from Rimah?"

GOD: "The first one. I just love Job. I'm very big on Job. I'm a huge Job fan. Job is very devout. You should see his burnt offerings. Lovely."

SATAN: "Of course he's devout. You give him everything he wants. But take away his kids, his big house, his flocks, the admiration of his peers and what would he be like? He only goes through the motions of being observant because he thinks it'll keep him on your good side."

GOD: (Appalled. Much like when he got the final prototype for dinosaurs.) "You think?"

SATAN: "The first hiccup of bad luck and Job would

drop you faster than you could say, 'Judas wasn't a team player.'"

GOD: "I don't believe it. Job's devotion is based on true affection."

SATAN: "What say we put it to a test? See what Job's faith is really made of. If you're right and Job continues to praise your name even when his life hits a few snags, I'll give you back Las Vegas. If I'm right and he starts cursing you at the first sign of bad luck, then you give me prime-time television programers."

GOD: "They're not yours now? I'll have to look into that. OK, it's a deal. You can take away everything Job has. But...you can't actually kill him."

SATAN: "By the time I'm finished, he'll wish I had."

Now, those of you who are thinking that this can't really be in the Bible, I assure you it is. And let me tell you, the next forty-eight hours for Job are nothing less than Biblical. A plague of locusts would look good compared to what happens to Job now.

ACT THREE: Cue the Sabeans.

The Sabeans were about the worst kind of people going in Job's area apparently. They "fall upon" Job's herds, carry off his sheep and oxen and murder most of his servants.

ACT FOUR: Cue the Chaldeans.

Next the Chaldeans show up and they're just as bad. They nab Job's camels and kill more servants.

SATAN: "How about we finish it off with a good ol' natural disaster?"

A big wind comes. It knocks down the house where Job's children are feasting and, most likely, holding hands and singing "Together Forever." All of Job's children are killed.

One servant manages to escape the wreckage. He drags himself to Job, bleeding, exhausted. The servant tells Job that his house, his wealth, his livestock and servants are all gone and his children are dead. Everything Job has treasured and prided himself on is gone. Mind you, we still haven't heard anything about his wife. I'm just saying.

Job does not scream or cry or wail. Instead, he says, "Well, I came into the world with nothing. I guess I will leave it the same way. Everything I had was given to me by God. I can't complain if God decides to take it back again. I still bless God's name."

This is where we get the famous expression "The patience of Job." The patience of Job denotes the quality of being able to endure extreme trials and tribulations without complaining. It means, "Putting on a good face in spite of the fact that life sucks." It is an accurate, meaningful expression except for one thing. Job doesn't remain patient for very long.

Job's friends arrive and sit quietly with him for a few

days. Of everything in the Bible, I think this is the passage I love best. Because, that's about all you can do for someone you care about who is grieving deeply. Just be with them.

Job's friends sit with him for seven days and seven nights. This just happens to be the length of a Jewish shiva, the ritual observance for a death.

My father used to say, "The Jews do death well," and I think he was right. Jewish funerals take place within a day or two of death. Then there are seven days of mourning during which the loved ones don't concern themselves with dressing up or cooking. Friends drop in with food. Or simply come and sit. A rabbi or elder of the synagogue attends to say daily prayers.

Shiva is a period apart from the world. It allows those who have endured loss to stay in their grief, let themselves be entirely engulfed by their suffering. Then, when the seven days are over, it's time to put the worst thralls of sorrow behind you. The mourners "get up" and slowly rejoin the community. The human spirit turns once more to hope and life. Writer Ernest Hemingway said, "The world breaks us all, then some become strong in the broken places." The best definition I've ever found for God is that God is what happens in those broken places.

So, Job is in mourning. He's lost everything. The

tides of fate have swept away everything he owned and valued. Still, initially, Job continues to declare his loyalty to God, which is exactly what God predicted would happen.

Then the first waves of grief pass. Suddenly, Job wakes up. He looks around and says, "Hey, everything I owned and valued has been swept away!" And, right away, he gets over being patient and accepting. Job is now mad as hell.

Job wails. He whines. He rants. He complains. He shouts at God. He declares himself the most hard-done-by person on the planet ever, ever, ever including well, everyone. No one in all of history has had such a bad time of it as him. Don't even talk to him about the enslavement of the Jews in Egypt or the sacking and decimation of Babylon. Not one of those enslaved, violated, displaced, massacred people endured even half the suffering that he's feeling right now.

On top of that Job insists he has done nothing at all to deserve this. He suggests that not only is life unfair but also God is unfair in really big letters. He says some other very bad things, such as offering up his wife (finally we hear about his wife and almost instantly we wish we hadn't) to be raped by the men of the town if it can be proved that Job has done anything at all to justify this misfortune. He cries that God is not good or wise or entitled to take back what God has given. God rewards evildoers and lets perfect and good men like Job suffer.

His friends soon get a bit tired of this. They have never heard of "the patience of Job" and wouldn't likely buy it now if they had. They say, "Hey, maybe you aren't so perfect, Job, or God wouldn't be punishing you like this."

Job rages. "I was perfect. I was, I was. I made my children pray to God for forgiveness even if I wasn't sure they'd done anything wrong. I was generous with the poor even though they're worthless dogs. I was the first citizen in the town. I was huge."

Job starts howling and complaining in chapter three (which begins, "Then Job opened his mouth...") and he keeps at it right through to chapter thirty-one. Seriously.

The interesting bit during all this is that we slowly come to see how imperfect Job really is. He slags the peasants. He makes it clear that his service as a city official was entirely about the prestige it brought him. Also, it turns out Job never loved his children as individuals. They were chattel, merely part of his status symbols or possessions, and insurance that he'd be taken care of in his old age. Job doesn't stop for a moment to consider what these disasters have meant to his wife. She has also endured her children's deaths, the loss of her home, security and position. Instead of comforting her, Job continues to rave that all the suffering is his alone. The picture we have isn't of a great, deserving man at all. Job is a sputtering, petty, egotistical tyrant whose spirit has been writhing in misery since long before the Sabeans showed up.

Finally, after many chapters in which Job whitters on about the unfairness of his life, Job's wife comes to him and suggests he commit suicide. Frankly, by this point, we're with her.

By chapter thirty-eight, God has apparently had it with Job's wailing and abuse, as well. And now something else happens that makes this story among the most remarkable in the Bible.

In a rare personal appearance, God speaks directly to Job. What makes this event even more special than the usual visitations of God is this. Every other time God speaks to someone in the Old Testament (God only has a brief cameo in the NT, a single line in the baptism scene), it's because God has a special mission to assign. Abraham, Moses, Samuel, Jonah, all were visited by God in order that God could present them with marching orders and deliver a "your mission, should you choose to accept it" sort of speech. God talks to people in order to let them in on their role in the Big Plan. Except for Job.

When God speaks to Job, God has no grand or even minor role in mind for Job to play. God doesn't tell Job to go preach to the sinners of Nineveh, or suggest that Job free Jews from captivity. God doesn't suggest that Job should build a temple, write some psalms or go out and father a great nation. God does not even exhibit any of the usual interest in issuing instructions as to what Job might have done to avoid his downfall or provide suggestions about what he might like to consider in terms of personal development in the future.

What God says is this: "Job, gird up now thy loins like a man." This is the Biblical equivalent of, "Put on your big-girl panties and deal." God says this twice, in fact. The thing about loin-girding, I mean.

Then God flashes before Job's eyes a resplendent moving-picture apparently intended to explain what God and the universe are really all about. It's a sweeping vision. A grand, shifting panoramic overview showcasing the limitless majesty and mystery of creation. The sight is magical. Awe-inspiring.

There are morning stars that sing. Clouds with the wisdom to know when it's time to rain or mist. There are storehouses of snow and hail. There are wild horses exulting in their strength and power. There's even a sea monster whose "breath kindles coals" and whose nose billows smoke and fire.

God treats Job to a display of the cosmos in all its facets and glories, a cavalcade of the fantastic and wonderful. It's all very reminiscent of a Beatles' song from their paisley period: riotous, psychedelic, yet somehow making absolute and perfect sense. And as he conjures up these extraordinary sights, God asks a lot of questions designed to prove that God is wise and powerful and Job...not so much.

Biblical scholars have fretted themselves silly about why God did this. Why did God choose to show Job these things at this time? After all, visions of singing stars and sea dragons don't seem to relate much to Job's loss or rage.

To my mind, this is God shaking Job by the metaphorical scruff of his tunic, saying, "Wake up, you idiot. Do you think you have any idea what life is about? Look at the splendour all around you. Think about the mind-blowing fabulousness of creation. And all you want out of life is comfort and prestige? Don't you think a God who can do all this could give you something better?"

This reminds me of an exchange I once overheard between my father and his friend Bob. Bob spent all of his time and effort amassing social status, property, wives, ex-wives, girlfriends, more social status, more property, very nice cars with ruinous insurance rates...you get the idea.

I recall my father once saying, "Bob, is this really what you want to be doing in your life? After all, you can't take it with you."

Bob's reply? "If I can't take it with me, I'm not going."

Bob is gone now. His stuff is still here.

Job, who is clearly an Old Testament version of Bob, has no idea what God's going on about. But he's smart enough to know that something is required of him. He cries, "I despise myself and repent in dust and ashes."

This sounds good, but God's not after repentance. God wants much more. He wants to give Job what he really needs.

Thomas Merton, a modern-day American Trappist monk said, "Happiness consists in finding out precisely what the "one thing necessary" may be, in our lives, and gladly relinquishing all the rest." Well, Job wasn't about to relinquish anything, so God decided to help him out. God took away everything Job had used to define himself. And, instead, offered him everything he needed to be happy.

For Job, as for any of us, that "one thing necessary" was learning to anchor his life and self-worth in things that endured and could never be carted away by the Sabeans. God offers Job the chance to leave behind the useless vanities and niggling little concerns of life and invites him to experience and rejoice in the vast, eternal grandeur of creation. And God offers Job the finest, most enduring treasure of all, authentic relationship with the great, eternal power of the universe. Which, of course, is love.

In a way, *The Book of Job* is the "Christmas Carol" of

Biblical stories, with Job as Scrooge and God playing every one of the spirits. Job has been treated to visions that startle him into seeing his life for what it was—paltry, shallow, empty, focused on things that can never bring true happiness or lasting comfort. And as the story ends, Job, like Scrooge, finds himself given a second chance to put his newly found wisdom to use.

God returns to Job everything he'd lost—his children, his position, his former wealth and more. But it's a different Job we see now. We suspect that while Job may enjoy his wealth and power, he'll always remember that it doesn't last and should never be depended on to determine his worth in the world. He quickly sets about proving that he loves and appreciates his offspring for themselves. He even arranges a legacy for his daughters regardless of the social custom that inheritances were only for sons. Job still doesn't mention his wife, but that just shows that there's always room for growth.

Let's go back now to that first act in the story of Job, the scene in heaven. I think God had the whole thing planned from the start.

ACT ONE.

One day, God was sitting around, thinking, "I'm concerned about my friend, Job. He's basing his life on praise and possessions. He doesn't see that these things are as solid and stable as grains of sand beneath the tides.

I wonder what it would take for him to realize that there's something better?" At that point Satan enters.

I walked home from church that day thinking, "I am Job." Not in owning tents and camels or disparaging peasants. I was like Job in that I too had a misplaced sense of what matters in life.

Years ago, I had a job running a theatre company. The chairman of our board of directors was a smart, successful woman named Jane, who had the distinction of being the first female vice-president of a major Canadian bank. Jane changed the way I understood my own value and purpose. She didn't dazzle me with fantastic images that spoke to the mystery of creation, though I was convinced that she had the power to do so if she'd wanted. Jane gave me one very useful piece of advice. She said, "Never expect anyone to say thank you."

At first, I wrote Jane's comment off as pure cynicism. But over time, I've come to see what she meant.

Like Job at the beginning of the tale, I can hand over to the world the power to determine my happiness and whether or not I'm of value. I can choose to define my worth as a writer by whatever a newspaper reviewer—when I'm lucky enough to get noticed—has to say. Or by how my friends and family tell me I'm doing. If I do this, sometimes I may receive the acclaim I crave and be able to keep my self-esteem afloat. But when I don't get it, and this may happen often, then once again I'll find myself drowning in a tsunami of the soul.

On the other hand, I can choose to make my purpose and the source of my value in life something the Sabeans of public opinion can never carry off. I can make it learning to write. Or learning to love. Or striving to know God and my own soul. Which, in my view, are all the same thing.

Learning to love and to know my own soul means that I approach each day with the attitude that simply to try is an act of courage. I can remind myself to take very small steps. I can choose to trust. Aim to be gentle with myself. Listen for that inner knowing. And accept that when I fall short, it's simply part of practice.

And, I can start giving myself better reviews. If not, "Anne is brilliant and talented," then maybe at least, "Anne tries. That counts for a lot."

If, at the end of the day, no one says thank you, or tells me I've done well, it won't matter quite so much, because my purpose isn't to please the world. My goal is to learn to know my own soul. If I keep trying to do that, well that's all I need to convince myself that I'm doing well enough. Slowly, no doubt with more than a few tumbles into the brink, I'm learning to paddle my boat.

Life is uncertain. Winds will come. The icy gales of criticism and self-doubt will sweep through our lives and threaten to wash away our sense of value and self-esteem. The water will surely rise and there will always be a tsunami of the soul looming somewhere on the horizon.

But if I make learning to love the star that guides me, and trust my inner knowing to pilot me through tempest and tumult, then perhaps the storms of life won't seem so severe. I'll be heading for higher ground.

IV
Losing Time

Pierogi in Heaven

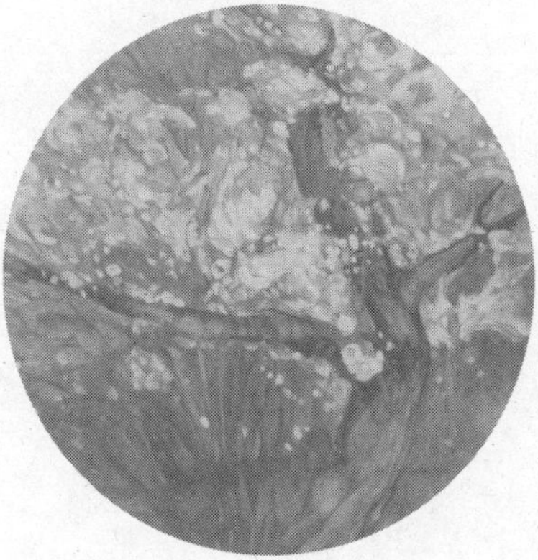

THIS MORNING, I'm sitting in my home office staring out the window. My workroom is on the second storey of my little house. From it, I have a view into the front yard that is cloaked by the sweeping branches of an enormous flowering cherry tree.

For more than ten years, at least five days a week, I've sat alone in this room, struggling to wrestle what I believe life to be, at least for the moment, into language. Outside, the cherry tree has been a constant reminder that wonder will always exceed words.

This tree is my companion and my calendar. In July, it unfurls an emerald tent, sheltering my little workroom from the heavy heat of summer. In October, its limbs are festooned with discs of gold, glistening and dancing in fall breezes. In January, snowflakes sparkle like sequins on bare black limbs, sending a shiver, which is not cold but rather joy, up my spine. By May, the tree is decked with blossoms, fleeting as first love. And in late June, buds burst into cherries. The ripe fruit draws blackbirds who chirp and jostle, disturbing my peace, dropping pits onto my car and smearing the sidewalk with a sticky red mess of sweetness.

When they were children, Jade and Becky coaxed their father to hold them high so they could cherry-pick. They yanked down handfuls of plump, ruby globes, dropping them into ziptop bags, then peddling them on the sidewalk like lemonade.

On warm spring mornings, like today, I make my first cup of coffee and go to sit on my front step. Early light washes across the roofs of the houses opposite, and my tree shimmers in lemon sunshine. The world bustles by. Dogs are walked. Neighbours trot to work. Children are led by the hand to school. The day is filled to the brim with the business of living.

In other years in this season the branches of my tree would have been lush and full by now. Decked out in masses of twinkling white flowers. But this year, the leaves came in sparse and patchy. Naked branches poke out amongst the green boughs. Blossoms hang in ragged clumps.

I love this tree. And it may be dying.

"Its just a tree," said a neighbour who found me standing outside this morning, shading my eyes against the sun, staring forlornly into ragged barren limbs. She walked off with her golden retriever. *Just a dog*, I thought.

I came inside and pulled out the phone book. I telephoned a tree expert. "Living things have a lifespan," he pronounced. Clearly it pays to consult a professional.

"You don't understand," I answered. "This tree is...it's my friend. It's the closest thing I have to a work colleague. You don't know what it's like to work alone and have only a tree for company." To his credit, he didn't answer, "Apparently it makes you a bit daft." Instead, he said, "Maybe it just needs some help. I'll come by later this afternoon and have a look."

So, I am waiting for an arborist to arrive and tell me the future. And as I sit at my desk looking out at my tree, I'm reminded of another lifespan and another friend.

A year ago, I worked as a volunteer on the palliative care ward of a local hospital. Two shifts a week, Wednesday and Saturday.

People have asked, "Didn't you find it depressing to be around the dying?" But our ward was more focused on life than death. There was always music on our ward, everything from someone in the lounge tapping out beloved hymns on the piano to a CD player blaring out favourite jazz tunes. Sometimes we even danced. Almost always there was laughter.

Once a retired opera singer, with us to live out her final days, asked to be helped out into our floor's hallway. Leaning on the arm of a nurse for support, she sang Puccini arias in tones of heartbreaking joy that carried to even the furthest rooms. Staff and patients wept with pleasure.

Every afternoon a volunteer pushed around a tea trolley laden with cookies and a good, English brew served in real china cups. Once or twice a week "Coco" arrived, an affable golden brown Chow certified as a "visiting therapy dog" whose preferred form of treatment was to lick everyone she met with delighted abandon. "Better than medication," we'd all agree. The small cares of life had lost their importance for our patients. The bills and bickering, worries that would now never become reality, they'd been abandoned at the hospital entry door. Instead, small joys of existence were seen and savoured. Sunlight through rose-tinted curtains. A card from a loved one. A sugary biscuit. A friend.

Still, on a palliative care ward there's no denying the reality of death. The people I served were dying. Not like the rest of us are dying, which seems almost theoretical on an average day. These people were with us to negotiate the final stage of life.

When I arrived to begin a shift, my first concern was to look on the blackboard in the nurse's station and read the list of names there. These were the patients who had died in the past few days.

Sometimes, seeing a name brought a shock. Someone I expected to meet again and to whom I'd said, "I'll be back in a few days. We'll talk again then," was gone. Other times reading a particular name induced a sigh of relief. A soul released from a body too long in suffering.

Patients were with us for anywhere from an hour to several months. Now and then, the combination of constant medical attention and rest did a client so much good they became well enough to go home. Usually this was cause for celebration, but sometimes a patient was sorry to be leaving a place that provided round-the-clock care and community. "They're shipping me off," I recall one elderly patient intoning, shaking her head, "I'm not palliative enough to suit them."

There are many patients I'll never forget. Louise, wracked by lung cancer, body frail, mind sharp as a tack, regaled me with stories of her long career as a journalist. The best times of her life, she announced, were the hours she spent drinking with cronies at the Toronto Press Club. One afternoon, I tacked a "Press Club/Members Only" sign on her door. We spent the afternoon sipping scotch (her) and ginger ale (me) and laughing over her colourful and cherished memories.

Andrew filled his hospital room with faux Christmas trees though it wasn't close to Christmas. Each tree was festooned with lights and tinsel, showcasing a different theme and colour: Delft-blue stars and moons, purple dogs and cats, bronze musical instruments, magenta purses and high-heeled shoes. The day after we did his twelfth tree, snowy-white with angels and feathers, Andrew died in his sleep.

Lucy meticulously charted her horoscope each day, her wizened hands scratching mysterious symbols onto large sheets of graph paper. Plotting her course. Lucy told me it was on account of my being a Leo that I would always "need to ask why."

"Now I'm Aquarius," she explained. "That's a water sign. I don't have to understand everything that happens. I can just relax and let life flow."

Katherine was with us for fourteen long torturous weeks, wasting away from cancer as her mother and sister had before her. Katherine stubbornly refused to take the dose of medication required to dull the crippling pain of her disease, insisting, "I'm not going to sleep away the time I have left." One day, I sat holding her withered hand as she trembled in agony. She said, "Most days, the wonder outweighs the pain." She gazed up through determined, tear-stained eyes. "I don't want to miss a minute of it."

A few days before Katherine passed, I wheeled another patient out onto the rooftop terrace. We came upon Katherine, skeletal, wrapped in a fleecy pink robe against the faintest of spring breezes. She was crouched over, gripping a length of garden hose. A bright clear trickle of water splashed from the nozzle onto her frail fingers. Katherine looked up, her thin face aglow with pleasure.

When Katherine died, I learned what happens to a person who passes away without friends or relatives to claim the body. It's sent to a city morgue for cremation. Then the name of the person is entered into a government record book. The extent of a memorial for a life lived.

Weeks later, I went to our hospital's chapel service, held for the families of those who have passed on while in our care. I went so that there would be someone to hear Katherine's name being read from the list of those who'd died in the past three months, someone who had known her. And to pay tribute to a woman who'd lived more fervently and died more fearlessly than I'd known was possible.

But today, as I contemplate losing my cherry tree, the patient who comes to mind most forcibly is an elderly man named Walter. Ninety-seven years old. Bent, hollow-cheeked, skin crackled like an overroasted marshmallow, but with eyes as clear and blue as a June morning. I bonded with Walter from our first conversation. He confided to me, "It's not the dying I mind so much. It's not having had any warning."

Smoking wasn't allowed in the hospital so I accompanied Walter outside twice a day during my shifts. I would roll his wheelchair onto the glaring asphalt desert of the parking lot, attempting to position it in such a way that from his hunched pose he could glimpse a tiny patch of parched impatiens that comprise the hospital's front garden. Then I would plant myself down beside him on a low concrete parking divider and we would talk as he puffed determinedly away.

Walter was an avid atheist, anxious to educate me, the

student minister, in the folly of having faith. "Don't believe that God stuff," he'd advise between drags. "Religion's the biggest nonsense there is."

I would gamely try to steer the conversation to topics such as sports, politics and whether food services might be serving the good macaroni and cheese for dinner, but we'd always end up back at a discussion of the unlikelihood of God and the futility of faith. Walter would ask me what I thought the Pope was up to. I'd answer that not being the Pope, or even Catholic, I really couldn't say.

"You're all in it together," was the retort. I had to admit that while this was the idea, it was, unfortunately, rarely the reality.

He asked, didn't I think belief in a god was just a crutch, a means of living in denial? I suggested that a man who had reached the age of ninety-seven and found that the approach of death came as a surprise knew something about denial.

"This spiritual stuff is for fools," he dragged deep and spit heartily on the pavement. I said I only knew that it wasn't for sissies.

Once, he wanted to know if I thought God cared whether or not a person believed in him so long as they've done their best to be decent people. "Not that I did that either," he said ruefully.

Weeks passed. Walter was now napping most of the

day. When I wheeled him outside, the sun had already crossed the pavement and now glittered against the cathedral windows of the neighbouring office buildings. The hot parking lot was cooled by early evening air. The small flowers were dim in their shadowy bed.

One particular day, Walter sat waiting patiently as I fumbled in my volunteer's smock for his cigarettes, dug one from the near-empty packet and placed it carefully in his thin lips. A few weeks ago he had done all this for himself. I struck the match and he breathed in painfully.

We sat in silence. I watched the pale reflection of clouds scudding across the corporate towers opposite. The afternoon business commute was over. The clamber of the cars was now so subdued I could hear the short painful puffs as Walter worked at his cigarette. It seemed strangely encouraging. The sound of life scrappily winning out against the odds.

Finally, he rasped, "I've come to a conclusion about this God rubbish." I waited. "What I've decided," he paused to hack loudly, "...what I've decided is this. It's easy to live without faith. But it's damned hard to die without it."

We continued to sit quietly. Deep shadows on the pavement washed closer signalling the end of the day.

"I don't think God, at least the way we've always pictured God, is for everyone," I admitted at last. "I think we've done terrible things to the image of the divine."

"Not what I'm talking about," he sputtered. "The thing that's terrible is what God's done to us. Like you take the greatest thing there is. Loving someone. I loved two women. And a son. Loved them more than my own life. They all died. The boy died forty years ago and to this day it's like someone's splitting my heart open with a razor. And now I still have to wake up every morning even though I can't go to the toilet on my own. I keep breathing and I can't even light my own goddamed cigarette. Everything this great, loving God is supposed to have given us gets taken away. Right down to our dignity as human beings. And what's supposed to make it all worthwhile? At the end of it you finally get to go to heaven. Where we'll all sit around having beer and pierogi and being happy. I'll tell you this. No amount of that can justify some of the suffering that happens in this world. So, if I was going to believe in some all-mighty creator who's up there running everything down here, there's only one thing I'd have to say about it. God sucks."

I thought about this. Certainly, "God sucks" was not on the list of "characteristics of the divine" that I'd been taught in minister's school. When faced with what seems to be inexplicable suffering, perhaps not caused but certainly allowed by our all-loving, all-powerful creator, the position of my seminary and my church is simply to insist, "God is mysterious." This sounds all well and good until you say it to someone for whom God's mysteriousness does nothing to lessen the pain of being alive.

And, why is God mysterious, anyway? Why can't the meaning of life and suffering be entirely obvious? Why can't this god thing make his/her/its intentions clear? In the end, it's hard to get around the idea that God may be all-powerful or all-loving. But not both.

However, I realized that as a seminary student and a future church minister I was called on to give my friend a sensible answer. And that there was only one responsible, reasonable answer I could possibly offer this man sitting hunched over from the burden of anguish and age. I said, "I think you're right."

My friend lived another two months. The last few weeks, he was too frail to go outside to smoke. I choose to believe that the hospital's painkillers deadened his craving for nicotine, but I know our trips outside were about much more than feeding his habit.

I sat by Walter's bed stroking bony, unresponsive fingers, sometimes singing softly. He died by inches. The last breath seeped out as delicate and unremarkable as a thin thread of smoke. I sat alone, feeling the room fill with the heavy significance of death.

It's Walter I think of today as I look out at my tree. It also might be dying by inches. And in spite of everything I know about lifespans, this has hit me as a complete surprise. It's hard to escape the feeling that my friend was right. It might be largely unspoken, but surely the one thing about the nature of God we can all agree upon is that sometimes, for sure, and in very big letters, God sucks.

The fact is that God, or whatever you want to call the perfect, infallible, all-knowing energy or presence that many of us believe played a key role in the creation of the world, really made an extremely botched job of it. For all intents and purposes, the universe is one gigantic cosmic Microsoft program—riddled with design flaws and with no effective course for complaint.

What we love is often lost. And in any life, pain and pleasure come at best in equal parts. Few of us will ever go to half the places we hope to go to or see half the things we long to see. Many of us will die with words left unspoken and dreams left unrealized. A successful life may, in fact, be one in which we simply learn to live with disappointment.

Some of creation's design flaws are obvious but fairly minor. Chocolate is fattening. We crave relationship yet most of us spend a lifetime learning even the most rudimentary skills required to be in one. The beauty and energy of youth is accompanied by almost entire ignorance about how to use it sensibly. And then, of course, there's February.

Some flaws are less obvious but more irritating. For instance, given the way the world is designed we're never able to truly dislike anyone. This is annoying because disliking other people is something I would really like to do.

Deciding that another person has no redeeming features is tremendously enjoyable. Recreational judgmentalness is satisfying. I say things such as, "Can you believe she did that? I would never do that." Or, "I cannot believe he behaves that way. I would never behave that way. He is a terrible, terrible person. I am way, way better than him." And, it feels like fun, fun, fun. My own personal *Jerry Springer Show* without the downside of having to watch the real Jerry Springer, which would quite rightly entitle other people to judge me.

Unhappily, self-righteousness is the all-dressed-potato-chips flavour of emotions. It tastes delicious, is instantly habit-forming and almost always leads to regret.

The moment you decide someone is too downright awful to live, this is what will happen. They will instantly do something entirely amazing, lovely and laudable that shows a whole worthy side you never dreamed existed. They might commit a small kindness or lobby to hold an office charity event. Or they disclose that they're fostering abandoned puppies or spent their vacation in some remote and Godforsaken slum building sanitary waste systems. Whatever it is, you'll be forced to admit that you were wrong in thinking they were entirely and hopelessly unredeemable. Worse than that, that you have something to learn from them. It's incredibly galling. Over time, I have had this sort of thing happen to me so consistently I've given up thinking I'm better than anyone else. It's just setting myself up for a fall.

There are other, even more glaring flaws in how life is designed. For instance, consider the process by which we learn our most important emotional lessons. There is an old expression, "We learn by experience." Usually this means, "We learn by enduring confusing, gut-wrenching horrible events from which, if we're lucky, we are occasionally able to eke out tiny grains of wisdom that may not keep the whole thing from happening again but at least allows us to delude ourselves into thinking it may have been worth it."

If the powers that be had arranged the world perfectly, there's no reason we couldn't learn crucial lessons by, say, taking a nice hot bath. Or getting a massage. Maybe just napping under a shady tree. If God wanted to prove God's great love for humanity, this would have been an excellent means of doing it.

Instead, we flounder, we ache, we puzzle, we curse. We creep our way toward self-knowing. Struggling to keep faith with a divine creator who decrees that a spiritually aware life is not for sissies. And that for some unfathomable reason, pain is the primary currency for life lessons learned.

All of this is not to say there aren't some real successes in how the world is designed. We have April mornings. Summer sunsets. Moonlight on new snow. We have the majesty of oceans. Falling in love. Kindness. Jane Austen. We have the original three *Star Wars* movies (in the most recent three, both George Lucas and God sucked). We have small children. The idea of heaven. But when you're in the midst of suffering, that may or may not lead to learning, none of that is enough. It's easy to decide, as my friend Walter did, that God sucks.

If you took a poll of every person in the entire world, the way in which almost all of us would agree that "God sucks," big time, and the most obvious, critical flaw in the makeup of creation is this: Human beings and all other things that live, age and die. Aging and death is God sucking in a big way,

To deal with this gigantic mind-numbingly terrifying mistake in universal design, humankind has developed an effective and finely honed coping strategy. We call it denial. Denial is what enables us to live in a world containing terrors ranging from earthquakes to epidemics, hurricanes to heartbreak, and yet still manage to get out of bed every morning, drink our coffee and head off to work.

My first realization of how valuable a life skill denial can be occurred about ten years ago. I was on the west coast of Canada, having dinner with my friend Marni.

Marni lives in a picturesque mountainside suburb of Vancouver. Over plates of pan-seared bay scallops with a reduction of organic balsamic vinegar, Marni calmly regaled me with an explanation of what was going to happen to her part of the world when the "Big Quake" occurs.

Marni's house, set high on the hills above the harbour, will come crashing down into the centre of the city. Then a tidal wave will smash onto downtown Vancouver. Pretty much at exactly the spot where we were sitting. The giant crest will submerge even the tallest buildings, towing everything not nailed down out to sea and turning the entire metropolis into a watery ruin, a modern-day Atlantis.

Coming from a relatively stable (at least where the earth beneath our feet is concerned) inland city, I was horrified.

"When is this supposed to happen?" I asked.

"Oh anytime," Marni said casually. "Within the next thirty years for sure."

I could think of only one response. "Waiter? The check!"

"How do you live, knowing this?" I asked Marni.

She shrugged. "You learn not to think about it."

Denial is humankind's natural defence against the indisputable suckiness of God's design of the universe.

We school ourselves and our conscious minds to simply solider on, ignoring the fact that death in the form of disaster or decay waits around every corner. Denial is what allows us to have such things as a booming real estate market in Marni's hometown of Vancouver or in places such as Los Angeles and Key West. It also ensures we have a cosmetic industry everywhere.

In all of life, there is only one circumstance that defeats us every time, regardless how skilled we may be at denial. One single event before which our ability to ignore and avoid reality crumbles. I am speaking, of course, of birthdays.

The summer I turned twenty-one, I learned the hard way that birthdays will always trump denial. I had a three-month job working as stage manager for a small theatre company on Prince Edward Island. This position was excellent training. It taught me at a young age some of the most fundamental truths about the nature of existence. Truths such as, "Life is weird."

Our theatre was in a tiny town consisting of a fishing wharf, a lobster restaurant, and a cornerstore that closed for lunch at 11 a.m. and often never reopened. That was about it, besides the ten or fifteen faded houses that lined the single mottled street, and a small schoolhouse that had been converted to house our company.

The leading lady and man for all of our summer

shows were two talented local actors named Laurel and Bill. Bill preferred to be called Izzard Goat. I don't know why. I do know it suited him much better than plain Bill.

Many stories circulated about Izzard, the truth of which I cannot vouch for. According to some, he had a minister's licence, obtained by sending in a coupon from the back of a comic book, that he used to marry people. He was also reputed to spend Wednesday afternoons sitting outside the vast, crumbling Victorian house he shared with Laurel and their many raucous, barefooted children by, again according to rumour, various different partners, dispensing advice to passersby.

In Izzard and Laurel's rambling shamble of a kitchen there was a poster that read "Peace is here. If you want it." I used to think, "So is insanity. Even if you don't." Izzard and Laurel were quirky, free-spirited, aging flower children, and two of the most interesting people I've known.

For a while, another member of our theatre crew, Dan, and I rented attic bedrooms from Izzard and Laurel. I moved out when another of their tenants began appearing upstairs every morning at dawn, planting himself on the foot of my co-worker's bed and serenading him (and me) by bellowing "Oh Danny Boy" at the top of his lungs. I can't recall who this guest was or what eventually became of him. I think I recall Laurel telling me that he'd come to the island to study the effects of the zodiac on Izzard and Laurel's compost heap.

If life at Izzard and Laurel's place was controlled chaos, at the theatre the chaos wasn't controlled at all. In all fairness to the company I worked for, professional summer stock theatre isn't always known for being either orderly theatre or entirely professional.

An actor friend told me that a summer company he worked for mounted so many different shows in their season and allotted so little time for rehearsal that most of the cast never had time to learn their lines. Actors are resourceful, though. This group concentrated their effort on finding handy places on stage to hide the script.

"It worked perfectly," my friend assured me. "When I did my speech that went something like, 'I've waited forty years to inherit my father's estate and I'm not going to be beat out by you, his new gold-digging wife,' I simply had to glance down and read it off the page I'd tucked behind the desk lamp. And, when I taunted the heroine that she didn't have the guts to shoot me, I positioned myself where I could see the sheet taped to the back of the Chinese vase."

Then came the evening when an assistant stage manager took it upon herself to clean the stage props and mixed up the pages. My friend said, "I was so used to stationing myself behind the sofa and reading off the page I'd pinned on the back, I didn't even notice I was saying someone else's lines." His fellow actor opened the prop book where she'd stashed her own script and began reciting my friend's part.

Oddly enough, it didn't work out too badly. Well, "Up to a point," my friend mused. "After I accidentally read the actress's line, 'I will kill you with the very gun you used to murder my husband!' I ended up having to shoot myself." This made things awkward for the performers who had to carry on. The play was a "whodunit" and, as the cast proceeded to sleuth out the murderer, one little girl in the audience repeatedly lisped loudly, "But it was suicide!"

Another actor friend told me about a summer stock production she was in that she described as "experimental/avant-garde/low-budget/performance art/fantasy" in seven acts. One night the stage crew got the order wrong.

"We came out to do act three and found the stage set for act six."

"What did you do?" I asked.

She shrugged. "We performed act six, then went back to act three at the next change. The audience didn't seem to know the difference."

At my summer theatre company, I quickly acquired my own arsenal of coping strategies. I knew, to the second, at what point in each show our building's electrical circuits would overheat, tripping the main power switch, plunging the theatre into darkness. I would trot down to the basement, position myself at the fuse box, listen for a startled cry from the audience, count slowly to thirty to allow the system to cool, then throw the switch and we'd be back in business.

I learned to talk farming and fishing with the fire marshal when he arrived for his monthly inspection. This not only greatly expanded my knowledge of such activities, it gave my crew time to race around unplugging anything that might raise official eyebrows.

I learned that if you want to know how a show is going over with the audience, you hang out in the ladies room at intermission. For instance, when I wondered if a small amount of swearing in a new play was offending our seniors' matinee crowd, I staked out the women's washroom at the first break. Two elderly ladies huddled together waiting for their turn at the sink. One woman whispered to her friend, "Did you hear what that actor said, Edna? He said, 'fuck.'"

"I know," her friend shook her head. Then she crowed delightedly, "Maybe he'll say it again!" They hurried back to their seats.

The heat in our un-air-conditioned lighting booth was so intense that our lighting technician, Johnny, and I had to resort to drastic measures to keep ourselves awake. As soon as I'd given my "two minutes to curtain, folks" warning to the actors, Johnny and I would race out of the theatre, down to the pier and jump into frigid ocean water. We'd drip-dry during the performance.

In spite of this, sometimes one or both of us nodded off to sleep during the show. One evening, just at the point when I should have cued Johnny to cut the lights and end the play, we were both snoring peacefully. Alone onstage, Izzard delivered his impressive final speech. He declared himself undaunted and fearless in defiance of the fates. Then, he shook his fist at the heavens and struck a dramatic pose, hands on hips, head held high, waiting for the stage to go dark.

Izzard continued to stand. Many minutes of increasingly uncomfortable silence ticked by. The stage lights still blazed. Finally, Izzard clutched his chest, gasped that he was having a heart attack and, "Curses on the gods for their revenge," and he staggered off into the wings. Art isn't easy.

By the time August rolled around, bringing my twenty-first birthday with it, I thought I had seen it all, knew it all and had figured out if not how to make it all work to my advantage, then at least how not to let it make me crazy. Which may be the best we can do. What I was about to find out was that while I might have figured out the world around me, I didn't have a clue about what was going on inside.

The play our theatre was presenting at the time was a

classic English murder mystery. A key stage prop was an aquarium that the director insisted must be stocked with two live goldfish. He thought it added that all-important "air of reality." The rest of the set included flats that shook every time a prop door opened or shut and a spiral stairway, the top of which, as anyone in the first twelve rows could see, ended in a ladder.

In the dénouement, the final exciting moment of the show, Izzard would stalk over to the aquarium, shove his hand in, pull up a "diamond" necklace and say something along the line of, "Aha!" or "You thought you could foil me Count Ruffenwisterhausen!" It was something like that.

Izzard's bit of business went uneventfully right up until the day before my birthday. As I remember it, Izzard arrived to do the show that evening announcing he'd just taken a refresher course in stage makeup and that he would now require an additional hour to prepare for his role as he was planning to cover his entire body in #42 Tuscan Nude. Izzard felt his character in the play would be the colour of Tuscan Nude. I chose to believe him and thought no more about it.

When I arrived at the theatre the following evening, I discovered the goldfish in the aquarium, floating belly up in the bowl. When Izzard dipped his hand into the water the night before, the makeup had left an oil slick across the entire surface. Our goldfish were no more.

I'd already had a miserable day. I woke up in the wee

hours of morning gripped by the sudden, terrifying realization that I was now twenty-one and had accomplished nothing with my life. As the day went on, the spiral of despair continued. I fretted that I was far from home and the people who loved me. And were sane. I had no idea what life was about and I was young and inexperienced enough to believe that other people did know this. I was currently enrolled in a Bachelor of Fine Arts degree at university, meaning that I had no future before me at all. To top it off I'd had one too many lobster suppers followed by lemon meringue pie and now my very favourite jeans didn't fit. When you're twenty-one, all this seems to matter a great deal. Now that I'm fifty...actually, it still matters.

Now, I had arrived to find dead goldfish. And, it was my responsibility to somehow breathe life back into them before the show went up in two hours. I recall thinking, "This is the icing on the birthday cake of my despair." And then, "Oh God, I'm also using bad metaphors."

I plunked myself down on the aged, petrified couch in the theatre's tiny, basement Green Room and I sobbed. I cried my heart out from self-pity, loneliness, futility and the inherent existential angst of existence.

Then, I did the only thing I could think of. I got out a hot glue gun and began trying to stick the squishy fish corpses onto the side of the tank so they might at least, possibly, from a distance, and if I kept the stage lights dim, appear to be alive. Frankly, this was not really how I'd pictured my life turning out.

Izzard wandered out from his dressing room aglow with a fresh, thick coating of #42 Tuscan Nude. There I was, his stage manager, for one brief summer his master and guide, standing in the Green Room, glue gun and fish carcass in hand, weeping as if the world was at an end.

Izzard said, "Um...I can't find my socks."

I indicated with a gesture of my hand and loud sniffles that his socks were in his dressing room drawer exactly where they always were. I returned to contemplating the emptiness and horror of my life and to trying to get the fish to adhere to the glass instead of sliding in a gummy mess down the side of the bowl.

Izzard stood, watching. Then he said, "Someone told me it's your birthday."

I mumbled something I felt indicated that this might be the case and that if he couldn't see the tragedy of it, I couldn't help him, could I?

Izzard continued to stand quietly. Finally he said, "I have wisdom to share with you. For your birthday."

I snuffled ungratefully thinking, "If you stick a hand slathered in oil-based makeup into a tank containing water and live fish, someone else is going to have to pay for it?" But I looked up, glue gun poised, fish mush in one palm, hopeful that I might hear something, anything, that would make me feel that life was worth continuing.

Izzard paused again. Then raised his arms up and out, sweeping the air as if with giant dove wings, turning his face upward like he was calling on all the secret, hidden insights of the universe. He thundered grandly, "I say to you, remember this. Remember this moment. Because not all of life will be this glorious."

I think if I were going to subscribe to the "God sucks" theory, it might have begun right there. Izzard's advice meant nothing to me. All I could see at that moment was the glaring reality of life: We age. We die. And in-between, we spend significant birthdays listening to the incomprehensible ravings of pancake-covered actors. Frankly, it wasn't very encouraging. I spent the rest of the night mewling over the unfairness of the world and the really, really stupid design of life in general.

The next day the inevitable happened. I woke up and it was no longer my twenty-first birthday. I remembered that I was young and healthy and would be going home in just a few more weeks to a place where people loved me and did not sacrifice innocent aquatic creatures in the name of character interpretation. And I certainly didn't need to worry about making something of my life quite yet. No doubt the universe was unfolding as it should. I called my friend Dan and we made plans to spend the day at the beach. I tossed some beer into a cooler, grabbed a copy of *Cosmo* and tripped out the door, confident that birthdays would never bother me again.

And they didn't. Until August rolled around last year. This past August, I turned fifty.

My friends say, "Fifty is just a number." This is like saying, "It's just a tree." It's just a number, until it's your number.

When you turn fifty, you don't wake up next day and find life is still dewy with potential and promise. At least I didn't. I opened my eyes the morning after my birthday and thought, "Goddamn it, I'm still fifty." Then, "And it's only going to get worse." At middle age, our traditional coping skill, denial, becomes less effective.

I told myself I was being ridiculous, but somehow, realizing I was now old and ridiculous didn't help. I reminded myself that there was still a great deal of living before me. My mother became an ordained minister in her sixties and a healing touch practitioner in her seventies. One of my favorite authors didn't write her first book until she was well past fifty and penned her best work in her seventies and eighties. And, after all, I myself once wrote, "Getting older is a case of mind over matter. If you don't mind, it won't matter."

But it's hard not to mind. Each time I look in the

mirror I have to face the fact that any trace of freshness or a girlish bloom is gone forever. The other day I tried to wipe away mascara that appeared to be smudged under my eyes, only to recall that I wasn't wearing any.

Years ago, I made a vow to myself that I was going to age gracefully. I would embrace the changes in my body as they occur. Celebrate the natural aging process of life rather than clinging ridiculously to the blush of youth. When I turned fifty, I decided that's exactly what I plan to do. In ten or fifteen years. Until then, I'm clinging for all I'm worth.

I've been alarmed to discover that getting older isn't just a state of mind. It now appears to be the state of my thighs as well. I don't really mind cellulite. After all, it's hereditary. Finally, something I can blame on my mother. But it seems that if I want to take a stab at regaining that nice comforting sense of denial, I have to maintain the appearance of youth and do something radical. I mean other than exercise or changing my eating habits. That would be too radical.

Clearly, I've reached that point in life where if I'm going to cope effectively with the obvious signs of aging and the inevitability of death I'm going to have to do something beside just employ the usual denial tactics. I need better ones. Fortunately, there's a whole billion-dollar-a-year industry ready to help me out.

The cosmetic business, what I like to call "Denial for Dollars," has probably existed since the first humans realized they were aging. I imagine some prehistoric ancestor stumping cave-to-cave peddling Miracle Swamp Mud, spawning an industry that would span the millennia.

I spent two years doing research for a novel set in ancient Babylon around 525 BC. At this point in history, Babylon was the wonder of the world. It was a city graced by magnificent public spaces and palatial private homes. The finest minds taught and learned here at the most advanced schools in existence. The Babylonians boasted sophisticated knowledge of medicine, architecture, astronomy, engineering, mathematics and art.

I was fascinated to discover that 2,500 years ago, in this educated, cultured civilization, phalanxes of male scientists and wise women were making huge amounts of money concocting and selling ancient versions of Oil of Olay. Consumers of both genders snapped up pricey vials of unguents laced with sandalwood and vied to purchase soft balls of wax infused with fish oil, crushed cypress berries and new milk that users were directed to "rub gently on face at bedtime to lessen the appearance of fine wrinkles." Men smothered their scalps in specially prepared mixtures of olive oil and the blood of black calves to ward off baldness.

Reading the lists of lotions and potions, promising "skin as eternally youthful as the goddess Isis," one wonders if these ancient creams and concoctions could possibly have achieved their claims of helping customers defy the process of aging. And, could these remedies have been as effective in ensuring eternal beauty as those created in our modern state-of-the-art anti-aging laboratories? My guess is that they were exactly as effective.

The fact is, no elixir of youth exists today any more than it did 2,500 years ago. But that hasn't kept every generation and culture in history from looking for it. Or from claiming to have bottled it and being prepared to sell it for a price.

St. Augustine, Florida, is the site of the Fountain of Youth National Archeological Park. The site was built as a tribute to Spanish nobleman and explorer Juan Ponce de León who, in 1513, was credited with being the first European to reach Florida. As the story goes, Ponce de León stumbled upon the area while searching for the fabled Fountain of Youth that he believed to be somewhere around Honduras.

The story is entirely fictitious. During his lifetime, León went to many new and exotic places and explored many uncharted territories, including wandering around the Florida peninsula for a bit before settling down to become the first governor of Puerto Rico, but no evidence exists to indicate he was searching for the secret of immortality. The allure of the legend of the Fountain of Youth is so strong and so ageless (unlike us) that the man is celebrated and remembered for an act he never actually performed or, by all accounts, even thought of.

The fact that León did not search for, let alone find, a Fountain of Youth does not keep tourists from lining up to dip into and drink from the fountain in the park that bears his name. I'd certainly join that queue. After all, the basis of any anti-aging strategy is the triumph of hope over reason.

Not long ago, magician David Copperfield announced that a spring on his private tropical island has extraordinary powers to restore youthfulness. He reportedly hired a team of scientists to test and confirm its amazing properties. To most of us, this sounds like an obvious publicity stunt. Still, people have begun flocking to the island in small boats, clambering to be allowed to sample the water.

Humankind's pursuit of endless youth ranges from the simple and sensible to the bizarre and extreme. Generally speaking, sensible is what we do ourselves. Extreme is what other people do.

You may call it hope, desperation or a necessary weapon in the ongoing battle for denial. You can call it not being able to bear looking into the mirror and seeing an impossibly older version of yourself staring back. Perhaps the only thing all of humanity has always had in common is the feeling that aging and dying are states that must be avoided, at any cost. In order to hang onto any vestige of youth, we're willing to part not just with money, but with far more precious commodities, such as reason and dignity. On my fiftieth birthday, I found that my own desire to deny the march of time had become so great, I was willing to sacrifice all three.

A little research into modern anti-aging aids proved that there are a lot of choices these days for dealing with the aging process. Just not good ones. In the case of my cellulite for instance, I can either take a sensible, healthy approach in favour of non-invasive treatment and a rational view of feminine beauty or what I choose: never wear shorts again.

I knew I didn't want to go the "nip, tuck and suck" route. Sure, I could get my tummy tucked or my cellulite siphoned but, eventually, I'm bound to think of something else that I'd like to have done. Probably before I'm off the operating table.

Besides, after looking into what is really involved, I found I have a fundamental problem with this kind of treatment. I can't afford it. Six thousand dollars for perkier breasts. Four thousand dollars for smoother thighs. One surgeon I consulted assured me, "It will change your life." That's true. I would be very, very poor.

What my research did teach me is that a big part of fighting the battle of aging is to look after my health. The age-old wisdom goes that if you feel better, you look better. No wonder I look fabulous after a glass or two of red wine. So, I decided not to do anything foolish. Instead, I would go to a "longevity and anti-aging clinic." There's practically one on every corner these days.

OK, yes, anti-aging clinic sounds a bit like a "Hold Back the Tides" clinic or "Make Yourself a Foot Taller" clinic. The philosophy of these places, though, is that rather than provide superficial temporary solutions to aging, they strive for "optimum health" for a longer life. In other words, they won't make me look any better, but they'll increase the number of years I'll have to look worse. It's something like that.

I found the brochure I received in the mail very comforting. It turns out that many, many people are choosing to buy this kind of anti-aging, alternative health service. Mind you, many people buy things such as Enron stock and garden gnomes, but that didn't faze me for an instant.

It was easy to see from reading this material that private health care is really more evolved than publicly funded institutions. This clinic not only offered health assessments and procedures, but also a full range of

European skin treatments. I can get a collagen anti-wrinkle treatment at the same time as I'm giving a urine sample.

There were inspirational quotes on the brochure, such as, "Medicine is for the people. It is not for profit," followed by a notice that missed appointments would be billed at a rate of one hundred and fifty dollars each.

You can't put a price on good health, but this place was certainly prepared to give it a try. A full assessment, not including subsequent treatments, was three thousand dollars.

For me, three thousand dollars is a lot of money. I was reminded of all the times I have approached the more expensive cosmetic counters, chanting the catch-phrase "I'm worth it," only to see the prices and decide, "Well, maybe not." Three thousand dollars seemed too much money to spend just to have someone tell me what's wrong with me. I have relatives who will do it for nothing. There were a lot of other things I could do with three thousand dollars, such as continue to feed my addiction to eating and having a roof over my head.

I opted for the mini-assessment plan, which cost four hundred dollars. For that, I would get a "biological terrain assessment" and they would check the state of my free radicals. I had no idea what either of those was, but it sounded very impressive. Before this, I would have said that "free radicals" was the name of a college political society.

From the clinic's website I learned that a "biological terrain assessment" is a computerized test that calculates the acidity, oxygen, nutrient and lead levels of my blood, urine and saliva. From another health website I learned that it is "total bunk." The argument is that any common blood or urine test will detect diseases or nutrient deficiencies. I was undaunted by this. After all, the world has always mocked those who set out to discover the Fountain of Youth. OK, perhaps for good reason. But I still wanted a "biological assessment test."

It also explained on the clinic website that free radicals are "highly reactive molecules with an unsatisfied electron valence." Apparently, the deterioration of my free radicals was likely interfering with the intervention of my antioxidants at this very moment. I was torn between grabbing the phone and immediately calling to make an appointment at the clinic, or using this as the plot in my first science fiction novel. I reminded myself that it was important to pause, take a deep breath and ask myself if an anti-aging clinic was really something I wanted to spend money on. I recalled the old expression "with age comes wisdom." I don't know about that. I do know that "with age comes desperation." I called and pleaded for the earliest possible assessment date.

The last thing I did was check out the credentials of

the doctor in charge of the clinic. According to the brochure, he had no clinical experience in traditional medicine but did have years of practice as a psychiatrist. This was helpful because by the end of the time I spent there, I realized that what I really needed was to have my head examined.

Before going to my assessment, I was asked to fill out many sheets detailing my current diet, exercise strategy and lifestyle. I found the lifestyle questions somewhat naive. For instance, "Do you have stress related to relationships?" could have read simply, "Do you have relationships?"

There was a nutritional information sheet, which advised me to eat fruit and vegetables, raw as often as possible. Apparently, cooking is not a good idea. I never thought it was.

The clinic also provided a "glycemic index" that ranked certain foods according to how they affect blood-sugar levels in the body. Using this informative chart I was able to learn that eating a big bowl of corn syrup is probably not a good idea. Certainly, the doctors who put this together had wisdom to share.

The chart listed glycemic index numbers for various foods and cautioned me to keep my daily total as low as possible. Sponge cake, my favorite dessert, rated a 66 on the scale. Chickpeas, which on my list of "things that contribute to my joy in life," rank somewhere below canker sores and blind dates, had a score of only 34.

There were no serving sizes indicated on the chart. If I wasn't fully prepared to delude myself, I wouldn't have entered into this process in the first place. So, I spent a few happy minutes convincing myself that an entire sponge cake equalled 66 points and four chickpeas were 34. This would mean, I could eat half a sponge cake and only score 33 points, making it a healthier choice than the four chickpeas.

The day of my assessment finally arrived. When I walked into the clinic, I could tell this was a classy set-up. My own doctor has a receptionist whose entire job description seems to be to ignore the people standing in front of her for as long as possible. Here, they had three receptionists doing that.

Eventually, I was escorted into an examination room and handed a paper gown. I was a little put out. For my four hundred dollar fee, I'd expected Donna Karan at least.

A young woman arrived to take my temperature and record my vital signs. I asked if she was a nurse. "Almost," she said. I asked, interested, what "almost" meant. She said, "I would be a nurse except that I didn't go to school for it." As someone about to have this person conduct medical testing on me, I felt within my rights to probe a little further. "What did you go to school for?"

"I'm a Personal Enhancement Technician."

I didn't know what that was.

"Manicures and stuff."

Now I only wished I didn't know what that was.

"I only do the outside stuff," she explained. "The girl who takes your blood did an actual course." I decided it was probably better not to ask what kind of course it was.

I will never understand the wisdom of sticking someone in a small room with fluorescent lighting, making them take off all their clothes, wrap themselves in a paper towel and then think you're going to get an accurate blood pressure reading. In this case, the young woman used a computerized system to do the testing. The machine hummed, purred, then beeped impressively and finally spit out my reading. I was starting to feel I was getting my money's worth. After that, the woman got out the standard arm pump and tested me again. "Because the machine is usually wrong," she said.

Next, I stood on a metal scale that the technician programmed with my height. Two numbers appeared on the screen: my weight, followed by 37. "That's your percentage of body fat," she explained. I said I was amazed. Particularly since, given only information about my height and weight, this machine had as much chance of determining my body-fat ratio as it did finding a cure for cancer or assessing the value of my stock portfolio. I asked the young woman how she imagined the machine could do this. She shrugged. "I don't know. But the number should be 22. You have to lose weight."

Now, I am of a body type classically referred to as "a little on the scrawny side." The only way I could drop ten pounds is by donating a vital organ.

Later in the assessment, a different technician told me that in fact, the scale measures muscle content. "If you're at 37," he said, "it means you have too much muscle." Damn it. My rigorous daily exercise routine of running down to the kitchen to get another cup of coffee had finally caught up with me. Clearly, the way to improve my health was to install a cappuccino maker in my workroom.

Finally, the clinic director assured me that the scale does, in fact, measure body fat. It does this by shooting painless electronic charges up through my body. Somehow, this did not make me feel better about the procedure.

The clinic also took fingernail samples, hair samples, urine samples, blood samples. I was beginning to think they should be paying me. At the end of the assessment, a nurse explained the herbal detoxification program I'd be on during the weeks that I waited to get my test results. She said I could purchase the supplements and supplies I needed from one of the three surly receptionists on my way out. I said, "But you don't know if there's anything wrong with me yet."

She sighed sagely. "There's always something wrong."

I went home and waited three weeks for the test results. Finally, the big day came. I was ushered into the office of the clinic's head doctor. The grand poobah of anti-aging. The purveyor of longevity and eternal youth. It was a little like meeting God. Well different than God, of course. God had created the flawed design of life that was responsible for my aging. This man was going to tell me how to stop that nonsense altogether.

The clinic director looked like a real doctor in my book. Mature, with salt-and-pepper hair, casually dressed in an expensive European sport jacket that was just a little rumpled around the edges and with soft lines around his eyes from nights of sitting at the bedside of feverish elderly patients or easing a woman through childbirth. Then I remembered that he was a psychiatrist. Well, he still looked like the national spokesperson for Compassionate Physicians Monthly.

The doctor and I sat quietly for a few moments while he mused over stacks of my test results. Occasionally, he sighed deeply. He flipped through some graphs, shaking his head in gentle concern.

First, he delivered the good news. Having reviewed the comprehensive data of their many tests, he was pleased to assure me that all of my vital organs are functioning. What a relief.

The doctor went on to say that my results showed I'm entirely healthy by normal medical standards. Then he wiped his eyes. He shook his head sadly. Unfortunately, he informed me, medical standards are not high enough. Nowhere near it. He explained that Canada's official *Food Guide to Healthy Eating* is useful for warding off scurvy at best.

He went on to say that my test results indicate that the rH2 value of my blood shows that the relative concentration of electron donors to electron acceptors has decreased. This is bad. Or possibly bad. He said it means that, at the age of fifty, I might now begin to experience a decrease in the functioning of my bladder and in overall muscle tone. This sounded like a pretty good bet.

There was good news. The doctor launched into an exhaustive outline of treatments designed to buck me right up. Vitamin injections. Water therapies. Something called "glandular super erogation regime," that I didn't really understand except that it seemed to involve having my naked body entirely coated with monkey spit and sludge scrapped from the underside of a dead tree. I spent a few minutes pondering how far we'd actually come from ancient Babylon.

I asked him, if I did all this, would it ensure that I stay healthy? "It's possible," he answered.

I left the clinic and rode down the elevator with the sinking realization I'd just spent four hundred dollars to be told that I'm a normally healthy fifty-year-old woman.

There was only one thing to do. It was time to admit to myself that there's really no way to stop the march of time. I might, however, be able to keep it from using my face as the main parade route. I headed to a drugstore to load up on skin care products.

"Matifying solution." I had no idea what "matifying" was, but I wanted it. "Upper lip repair." Previously, I thought my upper lip was the only place that didn't need fixing. "Anti-imperfection cleanser." "Wrinkle therapy." A complete skin regime ran two hundred dollars and only if I was prepared to forgo the "youth serum lip plumper."

I wasn't sure if my wrinkles needed therapy. I was beginning to believe I did. I stood in the drugstore aisle, balancing a basket piled high with potions that held out promises as old and worn as time. I began to wonder if I was really prepared to throw away more money pursuing a dream that's as impossible as it is ancient. Because whether the product being sold was blood of a black calf, an anti-aging clinic or "clarifying hydra-protection" cream, the label might as well have read "Totally Kidding Yourself."

Surely I would be doing myself good if I simply accepted that there is no Fountain of Youth. Carefully, I placed the tubs and tubes promising miracles back on the store shelves. I would stop spending my hard-earned cash on something I'll never achieve. Instead, I'd expend a little energy and brainpower searching for something I had some chance of finding. I'd look for a way to understand aging that didn't come down to "God sucks." As is usual in my life, I found my answer in an unlikely place.

✿

A Harvard professor recently published a research paper about long-term romantic relationships. You may ask what this has to do with the anxiety of getting older. It's not, "being in relationship ages you." In fact, he didn't touch on the subject of aging at all.

The professor was interested in what factors contribute to making a satisfying long-lasting partnership. He suggested that, contrary to general belief, it's not the restrictiveness of marriage that leads so many to fail. In fact, it's those very restrictions that make being in a committed partnership worthwhile. When couples are free to behave in any manner they choose with no regard for responsibility, social standards or each other's feelings, there's no impetus for them to consider what they really value in life. No reason to discover what being in relationship might teach them about themselves.

The restrictions of marriage don't only include the expectation of fidelity. There's also the constant requirement for compromise. Someone once described the process of compromise in partnerships as "a negotiation based on intentional, equal and goodwill decision making, where the end result is that neither party gets what they want."

What this Harvard professor was saying was something along the lines of this: If you "cut and run" every time you hit a rough patch, which in the average romantic relationship occurs approximately every twenty seconds, you'll never learn anything about the important underlying issues that are creating the conflict. And, he insisted, no matter how trivial the disagreement at hand may appear, there are always other, larger issues at play. Unless you stay at the table, you'll never get started on the difficult business of sorting out what these issues might be that will, in turn, assist you in truly knowing your partner and yourself.

I have an example of this. My sister, Keltie, recently entered into a significant and serious new relationship. She bought a cottage.

For Keltie, this was the realization of a lifelong dream. It's a magnificent cottage. Floor-to-ceiling windows open onto a panoramic view of a sun-drenched, wind-tossed lake. Majestic pines infuse the air with the scent of wildness and solitude. The quiet stretches for days.

Keltie has been yearning for just such a vacation

property for years. Two months ago, she took possession. This morning, she called to tell me she wished she could sell the place and forget it ever existed.

The dock, which seemed solid and stable appears on closer examination to be sliding sideways into the lake. The contractor Keltie brought in to have a look at it assures her the structure is still entirely useable. So long as what she uses it for is firewood.

He also cheerfully informed her that the beautiful sprawling main building with accompanying guest cabin and a garage, that could comfortably house a small fleet of aircraft, are all in immediate need of being entirely stripped, refinished and weather-sealed before winter comes. Or it rains.

Then there's the plumbing issue.

Now, at this point many of you will be asking the two questions: "Couldn't she have seen this coming?" and "Why doesn't she get rid of the place?" Perhaps also, "Is this contractor looking for a way to finance his own holiday property?" In fact, the man made it clear that while he was delighted to spend an hour pointing out everything that needs prompt attention, he was far too busy rescuing other people's dream vacation homes to do any of the actual work.

So, "Couldn't she have seen this coming?" Of course not. Keltie was in love. Beguiled by a spectacular vista.

Bewitched by the dream of what cottage life at its finest, most relaxing, most soul-restoring, can be. Just as we all at some point or other fall in love with an idea of what marriage and partnership can be and, for a little while, let this be more real than the actual fact of the person we're planning to attempt it with.

"Why doesn't she get rid of the place?" She can't. A recent slide in the real estate market means she'd never get anywhere near what she paid for the place. And she's obliged to find a buyer that her financial institution deems qualified to assume the remainder of her five-year mortgage. Bottom line, what the bank has joined together, Keltie'd have a heck of a time putting asunder. She's stuck for the duration.

Which leads us to a final question, "What the hell is she going to do?"

Well let's pretend, first of all, that Keltie decided she was prepared to take a financial hit and she was able to find a buyer. She could walk away from the cottage and write the whole event off as an unfortunate financial and emotional experience. In that case, what would she have learned? Possibly, "Cottage ownership is bad." Or "Be careful what you mortgage." Both of these are useful lessons.

But, because she can't "cut and run," Keltie is forced to confront difficult, uncomfortable issues. Frustration. Disillusionment. And what we really resent having to deal with, the reality of the situation. Faced with all this trial and annoyance, what might she learn? What might any of us learn?

Well, to confront frustration, disillusionment and reality for starters. But also, I think, to take on the challenge of rebuilding and repairing one small job at a time. This applies equally to cottages and lives. Keltie may also learn to let go of the illusion that there will ever be a time when everything is working perfectly. Also, possibly, she'll come to appreciate that achieving a dream is only the beginning of nurturing it.

There's an old saying, "The true gardener is not he who plants, but he who tends." Planting a garden is merely a first step. After that comes years of the pruning, watering and feeding. It's through that continual care and presence that relationship with the garden roots and pleasure grows.

For better or worse, Keltie and her cottage are in relationship. At least, for the next five years. In the confinement of that relationship she'll have the opportunity to tackle some fundamental, larger issues and to master lessons that can be applied to parts of her life that have nothing to do with docks or dry rot. She will do this because she doesn't have a choice.

I don't think the Harvard professor writing about marriage meant for a moment that we should stay in unhealthy relationships, no matter what. It's important to be aware of whether an alliance is fostering self-growth or self-destruction.

But in a viable healthy partnership, it's the boundaries that make nurturing self-evaluation not only possible, but also necessary. In order to figure out how to co-exist happily and respectfully with our partners, we first have to figure out our own selves. So, whether we're talking cottages or companionships, it's in the limitations of relationship that we have the opportunity to find meaning.

The same goes for my relationship with my life as a whole. Perhaps for me, going under the knife is a "cut and run." My best course of action is to engage in the process of living. Not only the parts I like, but also the parts I can learn from.

Above my desk hangs the poster of Van Gogh's sunflowers. The painting is a testament to the beauty inherent in life's imperfections. The sunflower blossoms are fiery and vital. But the deep curve in their stems suggests that, in not too many days after the painter captured them, the vase would be emptied. Bunches of poppies and cornflowers, freshly gathered from the hillsides of Arles would take their place. The sunflowers, whose portrait was destined to become famous, would be tossed into the compost to decay and feed the garden when spring returned once more.

When the sun slants low in the early afternoon, it floods through my workroom window, illuminating my poster. For a very few minutes, the light is at just the right angle that, when I glance up from my keyboard, I see my own reflection in the glass.

The first time this happened, I was startled to raise my eyes from the computer screen and find the face of an unfamiliar, older woman before me. The next time, I began tracing a finger along the tiny crevices around my mouth and eyes. I wondered if, in my own imperfections of baggy jowls and wrinkled neck, I might find meaning or beauty.

Like the stooping sunflowers, the gentle sagging of my skin tells a story. Not about beauty necessarily. And not about life as a whole. But just about my life.

In the soft creases by my eyes, I see the imprint of the multitude of times I've laughed. And a testament of how much I cried when my father died. Snake paths criss-crossing my forehead tell of the gut-wrenching fear I endured when my daughter, Jade, came out. And fine lines near my lips recall the tears of joy I shed as I began to see the remarkable woman she was and the blessings her transition brought. A few faint newer wrinkles might be from tears shed as I anticipate my younger daughter, Becky, leaving for college soon and the end of my days as a full-time mother. Some broader strokes I'm sure are from my great broad smiles the day I took hold of Liz's hand and we walked down the aisle of a church, so grateful to live in a country where love is considered too precious a gift to quibble about what gender it comes in.

On this lined surface I see a record of fifty years of having got a little too much summer sunshine, because it feels good on my face. Fifty winters of Canadian cold that speaks to me of home.

A friend who practises homeopathy says, "Our bodies are a metaphor for our lives." This body tells my story. The bulge at my middle announces that I gladly exchanged stomach muscles for children. The slope of my shoulders recounts a decade and more of workdays spent hunched over a keyboard. Perhaps my fading long-range eyesight may be encouraging me to begin to look within. And my disobliging digestive system speaks of my reluctance to let go of things in my life that I no longer need.

Some people hire tattoo artists to turn their bodies into living, breathing journals, chronicling the important events and emotions of their lives. I got all this for free. With my crow's feet and creases, I am performance art. A walking canvas on which the inner and outer journeys of my existence are drawn in lines more vivid and dramatic with each passing year.

So, knowing that, would I still want to erase this picture? Start all over with a fresh new face?

Well...I might go for a little Botox around the eyes, you know? What could be wrong with that? I guess the part about having botulism shot under my skin. And the hefty fee for them to do it. Frankly, I'm not sure which makes me more squeamish.

For the moment my desire to know what I look like keeps me from wiping the slate clean. And, these lines are more than just maps of where I've been. They also show me where I need to go. Each tiny channel and furrow is a visible cue, placed right where I can see it. They tell me to give up honing my skills of denial and to devote my energy instead to embracing the natural progression of life. And they remind me daily that it's time to leave behind the preoccupations of youth and begin to look for a purpose that can better serve me now.

Carl Jung said, "We grant goal and purpose to the ascent of life, why not to the descent? The birth of a human being is profoundly meaningful, why not death? For twenty years and more the growing man is being prepared for the complete unfolding of his individual nature. Why should not the older man prepare himself twenty years and more for his death?"

I would answer Dr. Jung's question with this, "Well, because death is icky and scary." Even those of us with faith in a caring supreme power don't want to prepare for the end. We might believe entirely that death is coming home to the loving embrace of God, but that doesn't mean we're in any hurry to get there.

Also, how do you prepare for death in such a way that takes twenty years? I could allocate all my worldly goods in about twenty seconds, and choose a funeral plan over the net almost as fast.

What Jung meant, of course, was that the work of our early years is to build our lives on the outside. This means getting the job, partner, kids, house, car and at least one or two impulse-buy small appliances. The work of our later years is to build our lives on the inside. This might include learning contentment or cultivating inner peace. It might be coming to know your particular version of the divine or practising unconditional love.

Put another way, the first part of life is for figuring out the world. The second half is for figuring out ourselves. I could see that taking twenty years. Minimum. Wrinkles are nature's Post-it Notes, reminding us that our "to do" list includes sorting out our inner Selves. The Buddhists say, "Human existence is precious and easily lost. Now is the time to practise spirituality with diligence." The lines around my mouth are like a string around my finger, making certain I don't forget that "the time to practise spirituality with diligence" is now.

Looked at in this way, aging appears less like a mean-spirited trick, a horrendous, universal design flaw and irrefutable proof that "God sucks." In fact, it seems like a fine idea. A gift. When I look in the mirror, my wrinkles whisper a reminder that youth has passed. But they also gently assure me that this stage of life holds beauty and meaning of its own. The time has come to stop concerning myself with the temporal superficialities of what's on the outside and to turn my gaze inward toward a new purpose, finding what endures.

Possibly, grudgingly, I'm prepared to accept that aging has a useful, even positive role to play in my life. But not death. Death is the end of aging and...well, everything else. There is no possible upside to the ultimate downside of life.

Having said that, there are many experts eager to help us make sense of death. If you ask me, calling yourself an expert on death is a bit of a misnomer. It's like calling yourself an expert on skydiving when you've never been up in a plane. No one who professes an in-depth understanding of death has ever actually done it.

Well, almost no one. There are a few accounts of people who've been proclaimed dead for a space of time, then revived and recovered enough to describe their experience. There are also reports, particularly among Asian Buddhists, of those who have remembered past lives. Some have actually gone to the villages where they said they'd lived and identified places and people they knew in a former existence.

When a Dalai Lama dies, a hunt begins for the child that embodies his reincarnated soul. If a child is found that recognizes certain personal items that belonged to the lama, he is hailed as the renewed human form of that ancient revered soul.

Typically, it's young children who recall past lives. Usually, these memories fade with time. But recalling past lives is not always confined to children. This I know.

A few years ago when I was director of a theatre company, I was invited to attend an arts festival in Denmark. I spent three days exploring the winding cobbled streets of Copenhagen, sitting in outdoor cafés in the harbour, drinking delicious overpriced coffee, wrapped snugly in one of the luxurious wool blankets these restaurants provide to patrons. Then, I headed south through the countryside to the tiny seaside town where the festival was taking place.

The morning I left Copenhagen, rain was teeming down outside the train window. Through fog-streaked glass I peered out at rolling pastureland awash in floods and puddles. Sheep stood marooned on tiny grass islands amid watery meadows.

The train compartment was chilled and damp. I

deeply regretted that the Danish Transport Commission didn't feel obliged to provide blankets as those fashionable cafés had done. I sat shivering, gazing at sullen, unchanging scenery, looking forward to arriving at my destination where I would check into the hotel and take a long hot bath.

The train pulled up at a small town a few stops before the one I was headed to. Suddenly, I found myself jumping out of my seat. I grabbed my suitcase off the rack above and raced out onto the platform. I stood watching the train pull off. Wondering what the hell had just happened.

The stationmaster informed me there'd be another train along in a few hours. I could sit in the cozy well-heated waiting room. Or, I could stash my suitcase in a locker and go check out the tiny grey sodden village.

"We have an excellent museum," the man suggested. "World famous."

I stowed my luggage and walked away from the station.

I quickly discovered that while this museum might be famous throughout the rest of the world, none of the inhabitants of the town seemed to have any clear idea where it was. I don't speak Danish. I have, however, travelled enough in foreign parts that I've mastered the universal language of hand gestures. This, combined with simply wandering aimlessly at last brought me to a large brick building by a bay. A sign read simply, "Viking Museum."

I purchased a ticket and went in.

The museum entrance was spectacular. The front door opened onto a second-floor balcony in a vast atrium. A towering two-storey picture window showcased the seascape outside. Inside, with the ocean as backdrop, rose the skeletal remains of an ancient Viking ship. It was a striking view.

I walked onto the balcony. I looked down through the atrium. I saw the sea and the boat. The next thing I recall, it was forty minutes later. I was outside the museum entrance sitting on a low brick wall, soaked to the skin.

Recovering consciousness, I sat blinking in the downpour. I was staggered by the same dismay I'd felt when I found myself standing on a train platform in a town I had no intention of visiting. I pushed myself to my feet and faltered my way back inside the building and onto the balcony entryway.

I knew this place. Not the museum, but the setting. I knew the boat framed against the roiling waves. I knew this stretch of rocky coastline framing the ocean. I knew them not from forty minutes ago. But from much farther back in time.

I walked slowly down the steps into the artifact exhibits. I knew what these things were for. The pot hangers, door latches, oar holders and other small tools. I could have told anyone tagging along beside me how a set of blackened metal rings were used, "You take a fire spit, you see, and you clip these overtop like this..." I knew the name of the man recorded as having owned the largest tract of land in the area. *But he didn't*, I thought. *It was his brother.* I felt I could easily have found my way through the village as it had been nine hundred years ago, without any assistance from the map displayed across a side wall.

I left the museum two hours later and caught the train. Sitting in the compartment, watching the rain continuing to fall, I tried to make some sense of what had just happened.

A friend who practises naturopathy and Reiki contends that human beings have "cellular memory." In addition to inheriting, through our genes, such things as height, eye colour, a tendency to certain health concerns and personality traits, she suggests we also receive pictures, impressions and even the memories of those who have contributed to our makeup. My friend says it's no mystery that I was drawn to that particular place or that it felt so familiar. Many people find themselves strangely and entirely at home in places they've never been before. I must have Viking in my DNA. Being in that town, seeing artifacts of my ancestors simply triggered memories that have lain dormant. I will in turn pass these memories on to my children. Along with other memories I might never know anything about.

A psychiatrist I know insists that "past life" memories are simply expressions of present life interests and concerns. He'd argue that I identify with the adventurous spirit of the Vikings and their intrepid nature and that I have a fondness for the raw ruggedness of Nordic scenery and that these affinities led me to imagine I have some more tangible connection with the people themselves.

The Dalai Lama describes death as simply changing clothes. So perhaps he would say that, for a moment, I recalled a former outfit.

A Hindu friend relates a story of a young man who went to visit a great sage and asked, "Mother, is it necessary to know what I was in a previous life?" to which the teacher replied, "If it is necessary you will know it."

What I know is that I got off a train in a small Danish town not believing in a life beyond this one. A few hours later I got back on the train, convinced that in fact, in some way, it must be entirely true.

I don't believe in heaven. At least, not a heaven as my religion has traditionally described it or as my friend Walter had pictured it to be. I don't believe in some distinct place where, when we die, those of us who behaved well on earth are welcome to sit about feasting on beer and pierogi or whatever our cultural equivalent might be.

Nor can I accept that those who have led less-than-stellar existences are doomed to eternal torture, in spite of occasionally wishing it on people who cut ahead of me in line at the ATM. It occurred to me years ago that no soul could ever be content in heaven while another was burning in hell.

But I have learned that where there is loss, there is also becoming something else. When my father died, I became an adult. When I divorced, I became capable of a real relationship. When my child transgendered, I was transformed into a cheerleader for hope and unconditional love. So, with the loss that is death, it seems entirely reasonable to believe that something else may begin.

If I listen to some experts and trust my own experience, it seems that what ends with death may be only the functioning of my physical body and my conscious mind. Of course this doesn't make it any less alarming.

The conscious mind, after all, is the diva of our physical selves. It can't imagine anything happening without it. Elizabeth Kübler-Ross said that the biggest obstacle to understanding death is that, "it's impossible for the conscious mind to imagine an end of its own life."

To which one can only answer, "Well...yeah."

This reminds me of a problem we were given to solve in my first-year university philosophy course. An exam question read, "There is a chair in a room. If you leave the room, does the chair continue to exist?" We were asked to list what possible questions this concept poses.

My answers included, "If you're not in the room, who cares if the chair is still there?" and "If you're so concerned about the chair, perhaps you might take it with you?" Needless to say, I did not do particularly well on that test. I did get a slightly better grade than my classmate who asked, "Is there a matching ottoman?"

The point of this exercise, I think, was to encourage us to wonder whether or not the chair had any intrinsic reality of its own or if everything that "exists" is just a product of our conscious mind. This is tricky stuff, particularly when you realize that the only way to figure out the workings of our conscious mind is to use our conscious mind to do it.

What Kübler-Ross was trying to say was that to her mind, no pun intended, we are each of us more than our brains. Some people call this "more than our brains" thing feeling, intuition or inner knowing. Others call it a soul.

Writer C.S. Lewis put it this way, "You don't have a soul. You are a soul. You have a body."

The conscious mind, used to running the show we call "ourselves," will not tolerate this kind of nonsense. It smacks of mutiny. The conscious mind prefers, "I think, therefore I am." C.S. Lewis might have said, "I am. And, at the moment, I think."

Perhaps what I experienced that day in Denmark was

indeed my Self recalling a former life. Or, maybe it was my soul slipping the bonds of this reality to show me that time is just an idea. What I do know is that while I can't accept the traditional view of heaven, I now live entirely open to the suggestion that what our brain accepts as reality is only a small part of what truly exists.

✿

Back in my current life, my day of anxious waiting has passed. The tree expert has been and gone. He spent a half-hour examining my cherry tree. He says that with an expensive course of pruning and fertilizing the tree might live another three to four years. If I do nothing, it will likely be dead in two.

I sit down in the kitchen with a cup of tea. I ponder my options. Maybe I should spend the money. Possibly, maybe, buy my beloved friend a few more years. But isn't life about letting go, after all? Maybe I should just accept that all things end and simply let nature take it's course. Which way should I go? It's like standing in the face-cream aisle all over again.

I try taking refuge in denial. "It's only a tree."

Sure, when it's gone I'll stare out at bare hydro wires instead of leaves and blossoms. But I can plant another tree—a new, young tree. In only a few years it will grow tall enough to hide the wires. Renewal is a natural part of existence. "Change in all things is sweet." I think Euripides said that. Greek playwright. Lived in the 400s BC. Wasn't that just before barbarians stormed Athens, sacked the place and destroyed the city? So...change was not so sweet. Except perhaps for the barbarians. I decide I ought to locate a Greek history book and set my facts straight. But I realize this is simply an attempt to distract myself from the issue at hand.

I get up from the kitchen table and go out into the front yard. A few neighbours are sauntering home in this late spring evening, thinking of dinner, what the kids might have for homework, whether there will be time to watch the last episode of that television show they recorded. Life things.

Down the street I hear a rhythmic thud of a basketball on a front driveway. Children laughing. Then the voice of someone calling them inside to eat.

The air is rich and sultry, sweetened by the perfume of lilacs, newly opened. Warm with the promise of approaching summer.

I step across my tiny front lawn. I stand beside my tree. I feel foolish. No one just stands beside a tree. One can sit under a tree, climb a tree, lean against a tree, but that's pretty much where reasonable tree-related behaviour ends. I recall that there are times when it's necessary to make an exception to what's reasonable.

I stretch out my hands, placing my palms against the coarse grey and black bark. A cherry blossom petal, loosened by a wisp of breeze, drifts down and settles on my bare arm. I wait.

The trunk is warm beneath my hands. Amber sunshine shimmers through the thinning leaves, dotting the grass at my feet with puddles of light.

I am waiting for the tree to tell me what to do.

This is not a reasonable thing to do, but I am more than my reasoning conscious brain. I call on feeling, intuition and that deeper inner knowing, to tell me what my mind cannot decide.

I sense a word. "Gratitude."

I don't know what this means. I know the definition of "gratitude," of course. "Being thankful and appreciative." It also often suggests the desire to return kindness for kindness received. I just don't know what there is to feel grateful for as regards my dying tree.

I think about the other losses of my life. A marriage. My father, when he and I were both far too young. My concept of what "God" meant. A son. My belief that I could be happy doing anything other than learning to love and to know my own soul. Smooth skin on my neck and forehead, for sure. Time. Some dreams.

Each time, I could not see what might fill the space left in my heart and my life, for one simple reason. It hadn't happened yet. But blessings came. As surely as spring follows winter.

Of course what has come after a loss isn't always something better. Though it was more suited to who I was now, after I'd been pummelled a little smoother by the process of sorrow, polished a little brighter like a stone tumbling in the endless ocean tides. And sometimes what came was better than I could have imagined. Finding my true love. Discerning my purpose. Standing beside both my children as they grow into themselves. Discovering that loss and life take you by surprise. And coming at long last to believe that this is a good thing.

I go back inside, upstairs to my little workroom. I sit down again in the chair I've sat in every working day for over ten years. I look out at the tree that has kept me company and lifted my spirits every day during all that time.

I feel gratitude. No one owed me that tree. It has been a gift. And when it is gone, it will have taught me the power beauty has to change the most mundane hours into windows on joy.

For myself, I am fifty years old. No one owed me a single moment of this existence. It has been a gift. And I will mark each birthday to come not as a step closer to the end, but as a celebration for each miraculous marvellous year I've already been given to live.

If there is a Fountain of Youth, an endless source of hope and wonder, which are the real treasures of being young, it is surely this. Gratitude. Thankfulness, bubbling up in even the frailest, most fearful of hearts as we see beauty or experience kindness. Gratitude for the experiences, aches, loves, dreams, hopes, losses and eternal blessings of being alive in this particular world. A wellspring of joy is rooted in our deepest truest Self that is called to the surface by the blush of a sunset or the feel of a child's head in our lap. Or today, at this moment, for me, as I gaze out at the fall of late spring light through the thinning leaves of an aged cherry tree.

It's in the limitations of life that we have the chance to find meaning. Through the boon and burden of aging and death that we may learn to live and to value existence. And it's in the sorrow of endings and loss that we remember gratitude.

Gratitude softens sorrow. At least, I hope it does.

In two years, my cherry tree may be gone. I make up my mind to cherish each of the few seasons it has left. To let it die in its own time. As I will in mine.

And then? Well, if there is, after all, a heaven anything like what we're promised by the old-time preachers, then my friend Walter and I will raise a glass of beer and eat pierogi there together. Not because that makes it all worth it. But because it already was.

Acknowledgments

The author acknowledges debts of gratitude to:

Liz Earley and Keltie Sim, always. My daughters, Jade and Becky, and all my family and friends, who graciously allow me to share their stories.

My editors, Kim McArthur and Laura Bickle. With thanks to Jade Castillo, Michael Hines and Rick Mugford for their input and advice.

All at McArthur & Co.

Author's Notes

This is a work of creative non-fiction. Some names, dates, locations and other identifying information have been changed. The names of the palliative care patients and family members in "Losing Time" have been changed and represent composites. A portion of "Losing Time" previously appeared in *A Year in HineSight* (McArthur & Co., 2002).

I have used the term "transgendered" throughout this book because it is the word most commonly employed to describe those with gender identity disorder, also known as gender dysphoria. A more accurate term is "transsexual."

Finally, in the essay "Losing Faith," I struggled with where and when to capitalize the word "god." For the most part, I have chosen "God" to indicate a specific traditional religious image of the divine and "god" when referring to what might be considered a more informal or less conventional image...though there are exceptions. My intention is not to suggest that any one image is more worthy or appropriate than another. I apologize for any confusion this may cause. Art isn't easy.